THE OFFICIAL

ANNUAL 2022

Written by Andy Greeves
Designed by Chris Dalrymple
Contributions by Dom Smith

A Grange Publication

© 2021. Published by Grange Communications Ltd.,
Edinburgh, under licence from The Football Association.

Printed in the EU.

ISBN: 978-1-913578-72-5

CONTENTS

5   Welcome

6   UEFA Euro 2020 Review

12   A Brief Plotted History of the Three Lions

14   Three Lions Records

16   Gareth Southgate Profile

17   Men's Senior Team Staff Profiles

18   England Men's Senior Team Profiles

24   A Brief Plotted History of the Lionesses

26   Lionesses' Records

28   Sarina Wiegman Profile

29   England Women Under Hege Riise

30   England Women's Senior Team Profiles

36   Guess the Goalscorer

38   FA Grassroots Plan

40   Spot the Difference

41   Goal Scoring Trail

42   England Quiz

44   Behind the Scenes at SGP

46   The Story of Harry Kane MBE

48   The Story of Steph Houghton MBE

50   UEFA Women's Euro 2022 Preview

53   Wordsearch

54   2022 FIFA World Cup Preview

57   Crossword

58   God Save the Queen

60   Quiz & Puzzle Answers

62   Spot the Players

WELCOME TO THE OFFICIAL
ENGLAND ANNUAL 2022

What a year 2021 proved to be for England's national teams. The Three Lions won the hearts and minds of a nation at the delayed UEFA Euro 2020 as they reached their first major final in 55 years. The tournament featured memorable victories over the likes of Croatia, Czech Republic, Germany, Ukraine and Denmark – you can read more about the matches in our review starting on page six.

It was a big year for the Lionesses too, with many of England's players representing Team GB at the delayed 2020 Olympic Games in Tokyo in the summer of 2021. Sarina Wiegman's side are gearing up for UEFA Women's Euro 2022, which will be held in England between 6 and 31 July 2022 (read all about it from page 50) while they have their remaining 2023 FIFA Women's World Cup qualifiers to look forward to later in the year.

We profile both the Men's and Women's senior squads as well as Head Coaches Gareth Southgate and Sarina Wiegman. Join us as we take a look behind the scenes to find out what happened at St. George's Park during England's UEFA Euro 2020 campaign where there is a guide to both teams' leading goal scorers and top, all-time appearance makers. Elsewhere, there are other features, quizzes, games and plenty more besides to entertain England fans of all ages!

COME ON ENGLAND
#ThreeLions #Lionesses

EURO STARS

England shone at the delayed UEFA Euro 2020, with Gareth Southgate's side becoming the first Three Lions team to make it to the final of a major men's tournament in 55 years. Here's a look back at a memorable summer 2021...

GROUP PHASE

ENGLAND 1-0 CROATIA
UEFA Euro 2020 Group D
13 June 2021 - Wembley Stadium

England laid down an early tournament marker with an excellent performance against 2018 FIFA World Cup runners-up Croatia. Phil Foden crashed a left-footed shot against the post early on while Kalvin Phillips forced a fine save from Dominik Livaković with a sweetly-struck volley moments later.

The Three Lions had to wait until the second-half to make the break through. Phillips evaded the challenge of Duje Ćaleta-Car before sliding a perfectly-weighted through ball into the path of Raheem Sterling. The Manchester City player slotted home on 57 minutes for his first goal at a major international tournament. Jude Bellingham came on as an 82nd-minute substitute for Harry Kane, becoming the youngest England player to feature in a European Championship finals match in the process at the age of 17 years and 349 days. The 1-0 victory was the Three Lions' first win in the opening match of a European Championships.

ENGLAND: Pickford, Walker, Stones, Mings, Trippier, Phillips, Rice, Sterling (Calvert-Lewin 90+2), Mount, Foden (Rashford 71), Kane (c) (Bellingham 82)

CROATIA: Livaković, Vrsaljko, Vida, Ćaleta-Car, Gvardiol, Brozović (Vlašić 70), Modrić (c), Kovačić (Pašalić 85), Kramarić (Brekalo 70), Perišić, Rebić (Petković 78)

ATTENDANCE: 18,497*

ENGLAND 0-0 SCOTLAND
UEFA Euro 2020 Group D
18 June 2021 - Wembley Stadium

The latest edition of international football's oldest fixture ended in a hard-fought goalless draw. There were chances at either end during the 90 minutes. John Stones headed a first-half corner against the Scottish woodwork while Jordan Pickford made an excellent save low down to deny Stephen O'Donnell. In the second-half, Reece James headed a goal-bound effort from Lyndon Dykes off the line while John McGinn cleared after a scramble in the Tartan Army's penalty area late on.

ENGLAND: Pickford, James, Stones, Mings, Shaw, Phillips, Rice, Sterling, Mount, Foden (Grealish 63), Kane (c) (Rashford 74)

SCOTLAND: Marshall, McTominay, Hanley, Tierney, Gilmour (Armstrong 76), O'Donnell, McGinn, McGregor, Robertson (c), Dykes, Adams (Nisbet 86)

ATTENDANCE: 20,306*

CZECH REPUBLIC 0-1 ENGLAND
UEFA Euro 2020 Group D
22 June 2021 - Wembley Stadium

Raheem Sterling was heavily involved in a bright start to England's third and final Group D match. The forward latched onto a lofted pass from Luke Shaw and lobbed the on-rushing goalkeeper Tomáš Vaclík but saw his effort bounce back off the post. He was to open the scoring on 12 minutes though as he headed in from a Jack Grealish cross for his second goal of the tournament.

Captain Harry Kane was denied by a good save from Vaclík as the half wore on while Jordan Pickford kept out a long-range strike from Tomáš Holeš at the other end. A 'goal' from Jordan Henderson was ruled out for off-side in the second half. The 1-0 victory meant Gareth Southgate's side topped Group D without conceding a goal.

CROATIA: Vaclík, Coufal, Čelůstka, Kalas, Bořil, Holeš (Vydra 84), Souček, Masopust (Hložek 64), Darida (c) (Král 64), Jankto (Ševčík 46), Schick (Pekhart 75)

ENGLAND: Pickford, Walker, Stones (Mings 79), Maguire, Shaw, Phillips, Rice (Henderson 46), Saka (Sancho 84), Grealish (Bellingham 68), Sterling (Rashford 67), Kane (c)

ATTENDANCE: 19,104*

Final Group D Table

Final Group D Table		P	W	D	L	GF	GA	GD	PTS
1	England (Q)	3	2	1	0	2	0	+2	7
2	Croatia (Q)	3	1	1	1	4	3	+1	4
3	Czech Republic (Q)	3	1	1	1	3	2	+1	4
4	Scotland	3	0	1	2	1	5	–4	1

KNOCKOUT PHASE

ENGLAND 2-0 GERMANY
UEFA Euro 2020 Round of 16
29 June 2021 - Wembley Stadium

A memorable atmosphere at the 'Home of Football' was matched by a pulsating encounter between England and Germany. Raheem Sterling curled a 16th-minute shot towards the right-hand-side of the German goal that was kept out at full-stretch by Manuel Neuer. Jordan Pickford made a good save from Timo Werner in a one-on-one situation at 32 minutes and did even better in the second-half to turn a left-footed shot from Kai Havertz over the bar.

The deadlock was broken on 75 minutes with a flowing England move that ended with Luke Shaw crossing for Sterling to score his third goal of the tournament. Captain Harry Kane got in on the act four minutes from time with a header from a cross from Jack Grealish to seal the Three Lions' first knockout victory over Germany since the 1966 FIFA World Cup Final.

ENGLAND: Pickford, Walker, Maguire, Stones, Trippier, Phillips, Rice (Henderson 87), Shaw, Saka (Grealish 69), Sterling, Kane (c)

GERMANY: Neuer (c), Ginter (Can 87), Hummels, Rüdiger, Kimmich, Goretzka, Kroos, Gosens (Sané 87), Havertz, Müller (Musiala 90+2), Werner (Gnabry 69)

ATTENDANCE: 41,973*

UKRAINE 0-4 ENGLAND

UEFA Euro 2020 Quarter-Final
3 July 2021 - Stadio Olimpico, Rome

England's one and only match away from Wembley Stadium during UEFA Euro 2020 took them to Rome as Gareth Southgate's men faced Ukraine at the Stadio Olimpico. The Three Lions made the perfect start as Harry Kane latched onto a pass from Raheem Sterling and slid in to guide the ball past the on-rushing Heorhiy Bushchan after just four minutes.

Seconds after the half-time interval, Harry Maguire headed a Luke Shaw free-kick beyond the reach of Bushchan. Shaw was provider once more on 50 minutes as he crossed for Kane to head home his third goal of the tournament. The icing on the cake was provided on 63 minutes as substitute Jordan Henderson headed in from a Mason Mount corner. It was Henderson's first goal for England in his 62nd appearance.

UKRAINE: Bushchan, Zabarnyi, Kryvtsov (Tsyhankov 35), Matviyenko, Karavayev, Sydorchuk (Makarenko 64), Zinchenko, Mykolenko, Shaparenko, Yaremchuk, Yarmolenko (c)

ENGLAND: Pickford, Walker, Stones, Maguire, Shaw (Trippier 65), Phillips (Bellingham 65), Rice (Henderson 57), Sancho, Mount, Sterling (Rashford 65), Kane (c) (Calvert-Lewin 73)

ATTENDANCE: 11,880*

ENGLAND 2-1 DENMARK (AET)
UEFA Euro 2020 Semi-Final
7 July 2021 - Wembley Stadium

England ended their 55-year wait to reach the final of a major men's tournament with an extra-time win against Denmark.

Amidst a thunderous atmosphere at Wembley, England went behind on the half-hour mark as Mikkel Damsgaard thrashed a free-kick from around 25-yards into the top of Jordan Pickford's goal. The Three Lions' response came just nine minutes later as Bukayo Saka put a teasing ball across the Danish six-yard-box. With Raheem Sterling poised to score, Denmark captain Simon Kjær slid in to top him but inadvertently put the ball into the back of his own net in the process.

Danish goalkeeper Kasper Schmeichel was in inspired form throughout the 90 minutes and made notable saves from Harry Maguire, Mason Mount and Harry Kane to force extra-time. In the added period of 30 minutes, Raheem Sterling was adjudged to have been tripped by Joakim Mæhle in the 18-yard-box and referee Danny Makkelie awarded England a penalty as a result. Schmeichel saved Kane's original spot-kick but the Three Lions skipper responded quickly to fire in the rebound and send his team to their first-ever European Championships final.

ENGLAND: Pickford, Walker, Stones, Maguire, Shaw, Phillips, Rice (Henderson 95), Saka (Grealish 69) (Trippier 106), Mount (Foden 95), Sterling, Kane (c)

Denmark: Schmeichel, Christensen (Andersen 79), Kjær (c), Vestergaard (Wind 105), Stryger Larsen (Wass 67), Mæhle, Højbjerg, Delaney (Jensen 88), Braithwaite, Dolberg (Nørgaard 67), Damsgaard (Poulsen 67),

ATTENDANCE: 64,950*

ENGLAND 1-1 ITALY
(ITALY WIN 3-2 ON PENALTIES)
UEFA Euro 2020 Final
11 July 2021 - Wembley Stadium

Buoyed on by the majority of the 67,173 crowd inside Wembley Stadium and a British television audience in excess of 30 million, the Three Lions roared early on in the UEFA Euro 2020 Final. Luke Shaw finished off a flowing England move, firing a left-footed shot from a Kieran Trippier cross past Gianluigi Donnarumma, after just one minute and 57 seconds. The wing-back's strike – his first for the Three Lions – was the fastest goal ever scored in the final of a European Championships.

After a strong first-half display from England, Italy became increasingly dominant in the second period. Lorenzo Insigne forced a good save from Jordan Pickford on 57 minutes before Leonardo Bonucci levelled ten minutes later, scrambling home after an Italy corner.

England's best effort in extra-time was a strike from Kalvin Phillips while Pickford made an important save as a cross from Italy substitute Bryan Cristante flew across the penalty area. In the ensuing penalty shootout, Pickford kept out Andrea Belotti's effort as the Three Lions lead 2-1 at that stage thanks to successful kicks from Harry Kane and Harry Maguire. Alas, Marcus Rashford, Jadon Sancho and Bukayo Saka were unable to convert and despite another save from Pickford, this time from Jorginho, the Azzurri ran out 3-2 winners.

ENGLAND: Pickford, Walker (Sancho 120), Stones, Maguire, Shaw, Trippier (Saka 70), Phillips, Rice (Henderson 74) Rashford 120), Mount (Grealish 99), Sterling, Kane (c)

ITALY: Donnarumma, Di Lorenzo, Bonucci, Chiellini (c), Emerson, Jorginho, Barella (Cristante 54), Verratti (Locatelli 96), Chiesa (Bernardeschi 86), Insigne (Belotti 91), Immobile (Berardi 54)

ATTENDANCE: 67,173*
*Attendances were capped at different levels during UEFA Euro 2020 due to the ongoing COVID-19 pandemic and various national restrictions that were in place as a result.

ENGLAND TIMELINE

A Brief Plotted History of the England Men's Team

1872
England took on Scotland at Hamilton Crescent in Glasgow on 30 November 1872, in a match recognised by FIFA as the first-ever international. The friendly clash ended in a goalless draw.

1924
A year on from its opening, England played their first international at the original Wembley Stadium against Scotland on 12 April 1924. Eddie Taylor gave the visitors a first-half lead but Billy Walker equalised for the Three Lions in the second-half in front of a crowd of 37,250.

1950
England competed at the FIFA World Cup for the first time, beating Chile 2-0 in their opening Group 2 match in Rio de Janeiro, Brazil on 25 June 1950. Defeats to the United States and Spain saw Walter Winterbottom's side depart the tournament at the group stage.

1968
Two years after winning the World Cup, England entered the UEFA European Championships for the first time. Sir Alf Ramsey's side lost 1-0 to Yugoslavia in Florence, Italy on 5 June 1968 in the semi-finals of the four-team tournament, before beating the Soviet Union 2-0 in Rome three days later thanks to goals from Sir Bobby Charlton and Sir Geoff Hurst.

1966
England's greatest footballing moment came as Sir Alf Ramsey's Three Lions beat West Germany 4-2 in the FIFA World Cup Final, staged at Wembley Stadium on 30 July 1966. Sir Geoff Hurst scored a hat-trick in the memorable final while Martin Peters was also on target.

1990
Having reached the quarter-finals of the FIFA World Cup in 1986, England went one round further at Italia '90. Bobby Robson's side topped a group containing the Republic of Ireland, Netherlands and Egypt and then beat Belgium in the round of 16. Two Gary Lineker penalties helped them to a 3-2 extra-time victory of Cameroon before a penalty shootout defeat to West Germany saw the Three Lions bow out at the semi-final stage.

1996

Football came home in 1996 as England hosted the UEFA European Championships. Terry Venables' Three Lions were in fine form, with tournament highlights including a 2-0 win over Scotland, a 4-1 thrashing of the Netherlands and a penalty shootout victory over Spain in the quarter-finals. They eventually lost an epic semi-final against Germany on penalties.

2007

England's first senior international at the 'new' Wembley Stadium saw them draw 1-1 with Brazil on 1 June 2007 in front of a crowd of 88,745.

2018

Harry Kane won the Golden Boot as England reached the semi-finals of the 2018 FIFA World Cup. Gareth Southgate's side progressed to the knockout phase of the competition with Group G victories over Tunisia and Panama. A penalty shootout victory over Colombia and a 2-0 win over Sweden followed before the Three Lions went down to a 2-1 extra-time defeat to Croatia in the last four.

2021

At the delayed UEFA Euro 2020, England topped Group D with 1-0 victories over Croatia and Czech Republic and a goalless draw with Scotland. A historic 2-0 round of 16 win over Germany saw Southgate's men progress to the last eight, where they thrashed Ukraine 4-0 in Rome in the Three Lions' one and only tournament match away from Wembley Stadium. They returned to London to beat Denmark 2-1 in the semi-final, a match in which captain Harry Kane scored an extra-time winner. England took a second-minute lead through a Luke Shaw goal in their first major tournament final in 55 years against Italy. Alas, the Azzurri equalised through Leonardo Bonucci in second half and won the competition 3-2 on penalties.

MEN'S SENIOR TEAM: CHART TOPPERS

Here's a list of the Top All Time Appearance Makers and Goal Scorers.

TOP ALL-TIME APPEARANCE MAKERS

RANKING: 1st

PLAYER: PETER SHILTON OBE
SENIOR ENGLAND CAREER: 1970-1990
CAPS: 125 GOALS: 0

Peter Shilton holds the all-time record for the most competitive appearances in world football, having played in 1,390 games during his 30-year career. It is of little surprise then that the Leicester-born goalkeeper also tops England's caps list. The player, who represented 11 different clubs during his career, made his Three Lions debut against East Germany in November 1970 while his last competitive appearance was in England's 2-1 defeat to Italy in the third-place match at the 1990 FIFA World Cup. In addition to Italia '90, Shilton was included in England's squads for the UEFA Euro 1980 and 1988 and the FIFA World Cup in 1982 and 1986.

RANKING: 2nd

PLAYER: WAYNE ROONEY
SENIOR ENGLAND CAREER: 2003-2018
CAPS: 120 GOALS: 53

Wayne Rooney was just 17 years of age when he made his senior international debut against Australia in February 2003. Rooney was one of the most decorated players of his generation, winning no less than 16 major trophies at club level while he collected the Three Lions' Player of the Year award on four occasions. He turned out for his country at three FIFA World Cups and three UEFA European Championships.

RANKING: 3rd

PLAYER: DAVID BECKHAM OBE
SENIOR ENGLAND CAREER: 1996-2009
CAPS: 115 GOALS: 17

Along with Billy Wright and Bobby Moore, David Beckham is the only other Englishman to have captained his country on more than 40 occasions. Of his 115 England appearances, 'Golden Balls' wore the armband on 59 occasions. The midfielder's 17 strikes for the Three Lions included a stoppage-time, 30-yard free-kick that secured a 2-2 draw against Greece in October 2001 and a place the 2002 FIFA World Cup.

RANKING: 4th

PLAYER: STEVEN GERRARD MBE
SENIOR ENGLAND CAREER: 2000-2014
CAPS: 114 GOALS: 21

A key component in England's midfield throughout the early 21st century, Steven Gerrard made his senior international debut against Ukraine in May 2000. He featured in the Three Lions' squad for that summer's European Championships and he was subsequently called up for UEFA Euro 2004 and 2012 as well as the FIFA World Cup in 2006, 2010 and 2014.

RANKING: 5th

PLAYER: BOBBY MOORE OBE
SENIOR ENGLAND CAREER: 1962-1973
CAPS: 108 GOALS: 2

Captain of England no less than 90 times (a joint record with Billy Wright), the late, great Bobby Moore skippered his country to their biggest success back in 1966, when Sir Alf Ramsey's side won the FIFA World Cup. To date, he is just one of nine players to have made over 100 senior appearances for the Three Lions.

TOP ALL-TIME GOAL SCORERS

RANKING: 1st

PLAYER: WAYNE ROONEY
SENIOR ENGLAND CAREER: 2003-2018
GOALS: 53 CAPS: 120

England's second-highest appearance maker of all time, Wayne Rooney tops the Three Lions' goal scoring list with 53 strikes in 120 internationals. Rooney's strike in England's 2-1 win in Macedonia in September 2003 saw him become his country's youngest-ever goal scorer, aged just 17 years and 317 days at the time. In September 2015, he equalled Sir Bobby Charlton's record of 49 goals for England with a penalty against San Marino and surpassed the tally a few days later with spot-kick against Switzerland. His last goal for England came against Iceland at UEFA Euro 2016.

RANKING: 2nd

PLAYER: SIR BOBBY CHARLTON
SENIOR ENGLAND CAREER: 1958-1970
GOALS: 49 CAPS: 106

Sir Bobby Charlton's 45th goal for England, which came against Sweden in 1968, saw him surpass the previous England goal scoring record which had been set by Jimmy Greaves a year earlier. His overall tally of 49 strikes saw the World Cup-winner maintain his England goal scoring record until September 2015.

RANKING: 3rd

PLAYER: GARY LINEKER OBE
SENIOR ENGLAND CAREER: 1984-1992
GOALS: 48 CAPS: 80

BBC Match of the Day host Gary Lineker opened his goal scoring account for England with a match-winner against the Republic of Ireland in March 1985 in just his second senior international. He went on to score 47 more times, which included six strikes at the 1986 FIFA World Cup, which was enough to see him claim the tournament's golden boot. He just missed the opportunity of equalling Sir Bobby Charlton's goal scoring record with a missed penalty against Brazil in May 1992.

RANKING: 4th

PLAYER: JIMMY GREAVES MBE
SENIOR ENGLAND CAREER: 1959-1967
GOALS: 44 CAPS: 57

Jimmy Greaves is the youngest player to have reached a tally of 15, 20, 25, 30, 35 and 40 goals for England. He took just four years and 187 days to reach 30 goals for his country – the quickest of any England player to do so – with that particular landmark goal being the final of his four strikes in an 8-3 win over Northern Ireland in November 1963. He averaged a goal every 1.3 games for England with a total of 44 in 57 appearances.

RANKING: 5th

PLAYER: MICHAEL OWEN
SENIOR ENGLAND CAREER: 1998-2008
GOALS: 40 CAPS: 89

Michael Owen announced himself to the global game with a memorable solo-effort - and his third-ever goal for England - against Argentina at the 1998 World Cup. A regular goal scorer throughout his Three Lions career, the former Liverpool, Real Madrid, Newcastle United, Manchester United and Stoke City man got a hat-trick in England's 5-1 win over Germany in Munich in September 2001.

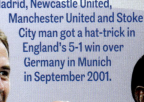

THE THREE LIONS' HEAD COACH: GARETH SOUTHGATE

MANAGER PROFILE

Full Name: Gareth Southgate
Date of Birth: 3 September 1970
Place of Birth: Watford
England Men's Senior Manager: Since September 2016

Gareth Southgate came through the youth system at Crystal Palace, where he was initially a right-back and then a central midfielder. He spent seven years as a member of the Eagles' first-team squad, becoming the club captain at the age of just 23. In 1995, he moved to Aston Villa where, within four months, he had become a senior England player by making his Three Lions debut under then-manager Terry Venables.

At Aston Villa, Southgate won the League Cup in 1996, before playing in every match of England's last major tournament on exclusively on home soil: UEFA Euro 1996. The Villa defender impressed in a three-man back-line. Unfortunately, his missed spot-kick in the semi-final shootout against Germany saw England go down to a 6-5 defeat on penalties.

After UEFA Euro 1996, Southgate's Aston Villa career lasted five more years, during which he appeared for England at both the 1998 FIFA World Cup and UEFA Euro 2000. He moved north in 2001 to join Middlesbrough. After a year, Southgate became Boro captain, and in 2004 he skippered the side to their first ever major trophy - the Football League Cup, which he had previously won with Villa back in 1996.

Southgate's final match in professional football came in the final of what is now the UEFA Europa League, where Middlesbrough were well beaten by Spain's Sevilla. Southgate retired having played almost 700 career matches, 57 of them for the Three Lions.

The Middlesbrough legend instantly became the club's new manager, replacing the departing Steve McClaren who had become England manager. Despite not having the required coaching badges, Southgate was granted an exemption and guided Middlesbrough to two midtable finishes, before ultimately overseeing their relegation in 2009. He was sacked in October 2009 despite the club sitting in fourth in the Championship and looking good for a potential immediate Premier League return.

After four years in football punditry, Southgate became England U21s manager in 2013. Then after three years, during which time he guided England U21s to the first of three consecutive Toulon Tournament successes, he replaced Sam Allardyce as England's interim manager at senior level in 2016.

Southgate became England's permanent manager following a promising first four games. Qualification for the 2018 World Cup was largely uninspiring, but when there, he inspired his side to a semi-final finish, where they beat Colombia on penalties to exact revenge for Southgate's personal penalty miss against Germany back in 1996. However, the semis were far enough for his England, knocked out by Croatia.

Southgate guided England to the top of their 2019 Nations League group, ahead of World Cup conquerors Croatia and fellow heavyweights Spain. At the finals themselves, England lost to the Dutch in the semi-finals, though.

MEN'S SENIOR TEAM STAFF PROFILES

Steve Holland
Assistant Manager

Steve Holland turned out for the likes of Derby County, Bury, Northwich Victoria and Swedish side Husqvarna FF during his playing career, but he had to retire through injury at the age of just 21. A year later, he became a youth coach at Crewe Alexandra, where he stayed for 17 years. Holland spent his last year at Gresty Road as the Railwaymen's manager, before spending a couple of months coaching at Stoke City. In 2009, he was snapped up by Chelsea, who handed him the role of managing their reserves.

Holland's two years with the Blues' culminated in him winning the Premier Reserve League and he eventually became involved with the first-team as assistant manager to André Villas-Boas. Holland remained in the role for six years, working under the likes of Rafa Benítez, José Mourinho and Antonio Conte. He was also assistant manager when Roberto di Matteo's Chelsea won the Champions League in 2012.

In 2013, he became Gareth Southgate's assistant at England U21s, fulfilling that job alongside his Stamford Bridge commitments. He left Chelsea in 2017 to focus on England's senior team as assistant manager.

Martyn Margetson
Goalkeeping Coach

Former Wales international Martyn Margetson played for the likes of Manchester City, Bolton Wanderers and Cardiff City in a senior career that spanned 15 years. Thereafter, he became a goalkeeping coach, representing a number of clubs including Cardiff, West Ham United and Crystal Palace while he worked with the Wales national team between 2011 and 2016. In 2016, Margetson joined the England national team as goalkeeping coach, continuing club duties with Everton and, since 2019, Swansea City. Martyn was England's goalkeeping coach during the 2018 FIFA World Cup, when the Three Lions won their first World Cup penalty shootout.

Chris Powell
First-Team Coach

Chris Powell played as a left-back for Charlton Athletic, West Ham and Leicester City amongst others in a lengthy 23-year playing career. He also appeared five times for England in the early 2000s. An experienced manager for Huddersfield Town and Southend United, he has worked as a first-team coach for England since 2019 and was assistant manager at Tottenham Hotspur in 2021, working under Spurs' temporary boss Ryan Mason.

Paul Nevin
First-Team Coach

It was announced in August 2021 that Paul Nevin would return to the England senior men's coaching staff. The West Ham United coach initially started working with the Three Lions in October 2018 as part of the FA and PFA's Elite Coach Placement Programme. Nevin remained with the squad through to the end of the 2019 UEFA Nations League campaign when England secured a third-place finish. The London-born coach, who previously held roles with Fulham, New Zealand Knights, Aspire Academy (Qatar), Norwich City and Brighton & Hove Albion will combine his England role with his full-time position at West Ham.

ENGLAND MEN'S SENIOR TEAM

(H) Home (A) Away (N) Neutral Venue

GOALKEEPERS

JORDAN PICKFORD
Position: Goalkeeper
DoB: 7 March 1994 **Place of Birth:** Washington
England Debut: 10 November 2017 v Germany (H)

Jordan featured in all 690 minutes of England's UEFA Euro 2020 campaign, keeping five clean sheets – more than any other goalkeeper at the competition. The Everton stopper has always excelled in tournament football for the Three Lions. He made a memorable save from Carlos Bacca to help his country to their first-ever FIFA World Cup penalty shootout success against Colombia in 2018. A year later, he became the first English goalkeeper to take (and score) a penalty in a competitive shootout while he also made a save as England triumphed 6-5 on spot-kicks in the UEFA Nations League Finals third-place play-off against Switzerland.

DEAN HENDERSON
Position: Goalkeeper
DoB: 12 March 1997 **Place of Birth:** Whitehaven
England Debut: 12 November 2020 v Republic of Ireland (H)

Dean joined the Manchester United academy at the age of 12 and was loaned to the likes of Stockport County, Grimsby Town, Shrewsbury Town and Sheffield United prior to making his senior Reds debut against Luton Town in a League Cup tie in August 2020. Previously capped by England at U16, U17, U20 and U21 level, the goalkeeper received his first call-up to the England Men's Senior squad in October 2019, while he made his Three Lions debut as a half-time substitute in a 3-0 win over the Republic of Ireland at Wembley Stadium just over a year later. He was included in the squad for UEFA Euro 2020 but withdrew prior to the tournament with a hip injury.

SAM JOHNSTONE
Position: Goalkeeper
DoB: 25 March 1993 **Place of Birth:** Preston
England Debut: 6 June 2021 v Romania (H)

A member of England's victorious squad at the 2010 UEFA European U17 Championship, Sam received his first senior call-up for the 2022 FIFA World Cup qualifiers against San Marino, Albania and Poland in March 2021. Having been named in Gareth Southgate's squad for UEFA Euro 2020, he made his Three Lions debut in a 1-0 pre-tournament victory over Romania at Middlesbrough's Riverside Stadium in June 2021.

NICK POPE
Position: Goalkeeper
DoB: 19 April 1992 **Place of Birth:** Soham
England Debut: 6 June 2018 v Costa Rica (H)

Nick has played in the Premier League, all three divisions of the EFL as well as the Conference Premier, Conference South and Isthmian League during his club career. The goalkeeper made his England debut in a 2-0 victory over Costa Rica at Elland Road, Leeds in June 2018 prior to travelling with the Three Lions to that summer's FIFA World Cup in Russia. His competitive debut came against Kosovo in a UEFA Euro 2020 qualifier in November 2019.

KYLE WALKER
Position: Defender
DoB: 28 May 1990 **Place of Birth:** Sheffield
England Debut: 12 November 2011 v Spain (H)

One of England's most consistent performers at the most recent European Championships, Kyle was included in the UEFA Euro 2020 Team of the Tournament. With over 60 caps to his name, the Manchester City player has regularly demonstrated his versatility in a Three Lions shirt. Gareth Southgate operated him at centre-back during the 2018 FIFA World Cup, while he also played as part of a back three and in his usual right-back slot during UEFA Euro 2020.

JOHN STONES
Position: Defender
DoB: 28 May 1994 **Place of Birth:** Barnsley
England Debut: 30 May 2014 v Peru (H)

A fine, ball-playing centre-back, John was another England regular at UEFA Euro 2020, who featured in all seven games and clocked up 679 minutes at the tournament. Previously capped at U19, U20 and U21 level, John played in all seven of England's matches at the 2018 FIFA World Cup and scored twice in a 6-1 win over Panama in the group stage. He was also included in the Three Lions' squad for UEFA Euro 2016 and the 2019 UEFA Nations League finals.

HARRY MAGUIRE
Position: Defender
DoB: 5 March 1993 **Place of Birth:** Sheffield
England Debut: 8 October 2017 v Lithuania (A)

One of a number of Yorkshire-born defenders in Gareth Southgate's squad, Harry scored in his second consecutive major tournament for England at UEFA Euro 2020. His headed goal in the 4-0 quarter-final win over Ukraine in Rome followed on from his strike in the 2-0 2018 FIFA World Cup in the last eight against Sweden in Samara. The centre-back came back from injury to feature in five matches at UEFA Euro 2020 – making the Team of the Tournament in the process – while he played in all seven matches at the 2018 FIFA World Cup.

KIERAN TRIPPIER
Position: Defender
DoB: 19 September 1990 **Place of Birth:** Bury
England Debut: 13 June 2017 v France (A)

On the back of winning the La Liga title with Atletico Madrid in 2020/21, Kieran featured in five matches for England at UEFA Euro 2020. He supplied the assist for Luke Shaw to score the Three Lions' opener in the UEFA Euro 2020 Final against Italy. Three years earlier, his perfectly executed free-kick gave England the lead in their semi-final clash with Croatia at the 2018 FIFA World Cup. He was ranked at the most creative player at that tournament, having created 24 chances in the six matches in which featured.

TYRONE MINGS
Position: Defender
DoB: 13 March 1993 **Place of Birth:** Bath
England Debut: 14 October 2019 v Bulgaria (A)

In the absence of the injured Harry Maguire, Tyrone Mings started in England's opening two UEFA Euro 2020 Group D fixtures against Croatia and Scotland, while he came on as a substitute against the Czech Republic. The Three Lions won two and drew one of those games, keeping three clean sheets in the process. Tyrone started his football journey playing for non-league outfits Yate Town and Chippenham Town prior to a transfer to EFL side Ipswich Town in 2012. From there, he gained Premier League experience, signing for AFC Bournemouth and then Aston Villa.

BEN CHILWELL

Position: Defender
DoB: 21 December 1996 **Place of Birth:** Milton Keynes
England Debut: 11 September 2018 v Switzerland (H)

Ben was an unused substitute for England during UEFA Euro 2020. Manager Gareth Southgate praised the Chelsea defender and the other players who didn't get to feature during the tournament for helping create such a good spirit in the camp. Ben had 14 senior caps to his name at the time of writing, which included a start in the Three Lions' UEFA Nations League semi-final against the Netherlands in June 2019.

LUKE SHAW

Position: Defender
DoB: 12 July 1995 **Place of Birth:** Kingston-upon-Thames
England Debut: 5 March 2014 v Denmark (H)

One of England's undoubted stars of UEFA Euro 2020, Luke made three assists in six appearances during the tournament and scored a memorable goal in the final against Italy with the game less than two minutes old. Shaw made his breakthrough into the England senior team whilst playing his club football at Southampton. His Three Lions debut came at his then home ground, St Mary's Stadium, in 2014. He joined Manchester United from Saints later that year.

REECE JAMES

Position: Defender
DoB: 8 December 1999 **Place of Birth:** Redbridge
England Debut: 8 October 2020 v Wales (H)

Part of the Young Lions squad which won the 2017 UEFA European U19 Championship, Reece made his senior breakthrough with England during the 2020/21 season. Having made six appearances prior to UEFA Euro 2020, the right-back started his first senior tournament match for the Three Lions against Scotland in the group stage of the competition.

CONOR COADY

Position: Defender
DoB: 25 February 1993 **Place of Birth:** St Helens
England Debut: 8 September 2020 v Denmark (A)

Prior to making his senior debut for the Three Lions, Conor represented England at all levels between U16 and U20 and captained the U17s to UEFA European U17 Championship glory back in 2010. A product of Liverpool's youth academy, the defender played at the 2013 FIFA U20 World Cup in Turkey alongside the likes of Harry Kane, John Stones, Ross Barkley and Eric Dier. His senior debut against Denmark saw him become the first Wolverhampton Wanderers player to represent England since Steve Bull in 1990. His first international goal came in a 3-0 win over Wales at Wembley Stadium in October 2020.

BEN WHITE

Position: Defender
Date of Birth: 8 October 1997 **Place of Birth:** Poole
England Debut: 2 June 2021 v Austria (H)

Ben was included Gareth Southgate's provisional 33-man squad for UEFA Euro 2020 and later made the final 26 following an injury to Trent Alexander-Arnold. Ben's Three Lions debut came in the run-up to the tournament as he came on as a substitute for Jack Grealish in the 1-0 victory over Austria at Middlesbrough's Riverside Stadium. He started for England four days later in a 1-0 win against Romania. The defender signed for Arsenal from Brighton & Hove Albion in the summer of 2021.

JUDE BELLINGHAM
Position: Midfielder
DoB: 23 June 2003   Place of Birth: Stourbridge
England Debut: 12 November 2020 v Republic of Ireland (H)

When he came on to replace Harry Kane as an 82nd-minute substitute at the age of 17 years and 349 days in England's opening UEFA Euro 2020 group match against Croatia, Jude became the youngest player to represent the Three Lions at major tournament. He briefly set the record as the European Championship's youngest player too, prior to Kacper Kozłowski featuring for Poland against Spain just six days later at the age of 17 years and 246 days.

JORDAN HENDERSON
Position: Midfielder
DoB: 17 June 1990   Place of Birth: Sunderland
England Debut: 17 November 2010 v France (H)

There was a special moment for Jordan at UEFA Euro 2020 when he scored his first England goal on the occasion of his 62nd senior international appearance in the 4-0 win over Ukraine in Rome. The Three Lions vice-captain appeared in five matches at the tournament, often coming on as a substitute to help Gareth Southgate's side see out their victories of the likes of Czech Republic, Germany, Ukraine and Denmark, while he also came on in the final against Italy. A two-time England Player of the Year, Jordan had previously represented his country at the 2014 and 2018 FIFA World Cups as well as UEFA Euro 2012 and 2016.

JESSE LINGARD
Position: Midfielder
DoB: 15 December 1992   Place of Birth: Warrington
England Debut: 8 October 2016 v Malta (H)

Jesse made his England debut in Gareth Southgate's first match in charge of the national team – a 2-0 victory against Malta in October 2016. The pair had previously worked together at U21 level, with ten of Lingard's eleven caps for the Young Lions coming under Gareth's management. The attacking-midfielder has scored a number of notable goals in an England shirt, including a strike in the 6-1 triumph over Panama at the 2018 FIFA World Cup and the equaliser in a 2-1 triumph over Croatia in November 2018 which saw the Three Lions qualify for the UEFA Nations League finals.

DECLAN RICE
Position: Midfielder
DoB: 14 January 1999   Place of Birth: Kingston-upon-Thames
England Debut: 22 March 2019 v Czech Republic (H)

Declan featured in all seven of England's matches at UEFA Euro 2020 with 538 minutes on the pitch in total. Since switching his international allegiance from the Republic of Ireland to England in February 2019, the midfielder has made over 20 appearances for the Three Lions, including playing 105 minutes of the UEFA Nations League semi-final against the Netherlands in 2019, in which the Dutch triumphed 3-1 in extra-time.

ERIC DIER
Position: Midfielder
DoB: 15 January 1994   Place of Birth: Cheltenham
England Debut: 13 November 2015 v Spain (A)

Eric scored England's winning penalty in the Three Lions' memorable 4-3 penalty shootout victory over Columbia in a 2018 FIFA World Cup round of 16 match. The versatile player, who is able to operate in either defence or midfield, scored his first international goal as he hit the winner in a 3-2 triumph over Germany in March 2016. Eric's 40th England cap came in the UEFA Nations League third-place play-off against Switzerland in June 2019.

MASON MOUNT
Position: Midfielder
DoB: 10 January 1999 Place of Birth: Portsmouth
England Debut: 6 September 2019 v Bulgaria (H)

Mason was a key figure for England at UEFA Euro 2020, featuring in five tournament matches. He supplied the assist for Jordan Henderson's goal in the 4-0 win over Ukraine in the quarter-finals with a fine out-swinging corner. A product of Chelsea's youth academy, Mason represented England at various levels between U16 and U21 and was named 'Golden Player' (player of the tournament) at the 2017 UEFA European Under-19 Championships – a tournament the Young Lions won.

PHIL FODEN
Position: Midfielder
DoB: 28 May 2000 Place of Birth: Stockport
England Debut: 5 September 2020 v Iceland (A)

Phil started in England's 1-0 win over Croatia in their opening match at UEFA Euro 2020 and also featured in two other tournament games. His summer exploits for the Three Lions came on the back of a wonderful 2020/21 season with Manchester City that saw him win the Premier League and EFL Cup while he collected the PFA Young Player of the Season award. Phil's first goals for the Three Lions came during the campaign as he bagged a brace in a 4-0 UEFA Nations League victory over Iceland at Wembley Stadium in November 2020.

BUKAYO SAKA
Position: Midfielder
DoB: 5 September 2001 Place of Birth: London
England Debut: 8 October 2020 v Wales (H)

Having previously represented England at U16, U17, U18, U19 and U21 level, Bukayo made his breakthrough at senior level during the 2020/21 season. Having made Gareth Southgate's 26-man squad for UEFA Euro 2020, he scored his first international goal in a 1-0 triumph over Austria in June 2021 in a friendly at Middlesbrough's Riverside Stadium prior to the tournament getting underway. He was named Man of the Match for his performance against Czech Republic in England's final Group D match – one of four fixtures in which he featured during the competition.

JACK GREALISH
Position: Midfielder
DoB: 10 September 1995 Place of Birth: Birmingham
England Debut: 8 September 2020 v Denmark (A)

Jack made two assists in five UEFA Euro 2020 appearances, setting up Raheem Sterling's winner against Czech Republic and Harry Kane's header against Germany. Previously capped by the Republic of Ireland at U17, U18 and U21 level, the Birmingham-born player switched international allegiance in order to represent the country of his birth at U21 and senior level.

KALVIN PHILLIPS
Position: Midfielder
DoB: 2 December 1995 Place of Birth: Leeds
England Debut: 8 September 2020 v Denmark (A)

Like Bukayo Saka, Jack Grealish, Phil Foden and Jude Bellingham, 2020/21 was Kalvin's breakthrough season at senior international level. When he made his England debut against Denmark in the UEFA Nations League, he became just the third player of the 21st century to represent the Three Lions prior to playing in a top division of club football (although he lined up for Leeds United in a Premier League match just four days later!) Kalvin featured in all seven matches for the Three Lions at UEFA Euro 2020.

RAHEEM STERLING

Position: Forward
DoB: 8 December 1994 **Place of Birth:** Kingston, Jamaica
England Debut: 14 November 2012 v Sweden (A)

Raheem's performances at UEFA Euro 2020, in which he scored three goals and made one assist in seven matches, saw him named in the Team of the Tournament. The forward, who was also included in England's squads for the 2014 and 2018 FIFA World Cups, UEFA Euro 2016 and the UEFA Nations League finals in 2019, scored his first international goal in a 4-0 victory over Lithuania in March 2015. He bagged a memorable brace in a 3-2 away win in Spain in October 2018. His first international hat-trick meanwhile came in the 5-0 demolition of the Czech Republic in March 2019.

HARRY KANE

Position: Forward
DoB: 28 July 1993 **Place of Birth:** London
England Debut: 27 March 2015 v Lithuania (H)

Harry's four strikes at UEFA Euro 2020 took him to within 15 goals of levelling Wayne Rooney's all-time scoring record of 53 for England. The Three Lions skipper netted in knockout phase victories over Germany and Denmark while he got a brace in the 4-0 quarter-final triumph against Ukraine. Harry's goal scoring exploits for England are nothing new. He netted after just 80 seconds of his senior international debut against Lithuania in March 2015 having come on as a substitute for Rooney. He won the Golden Boot award at the 2018 FIFA World Cup with six strikes in as many games while he was the top goal scorer in UEFA Euro 2020 qualifying with 12 strikes in eight matches.

MARCUS RASHFORD

Position: Forward
DoB: 31 October 1997 **Place of Birth:** Manchester
England debut: 27 May 2016 v Australia (H)

An inspiring figure on and off the pitch, Marcus became the youngest player ever to score on his England debut, netting in the Three Lions' 2-1 victory over Australia at Sunderland AFC's Stadium of Light in May 2016 at the age of 18 years and 208 days. The Manchester United forward scored three goals in qualification for UEFA Euro 2020 with strikes against Bulgaria (away), Montenegro (home) and Kosovo (away). He went on to make five appearances at the finals of the tournament, having previously represented England at UEFA Euro 2016 and the 2018 FIFA World Cup.

JADON SANCHO

Position: Forward
DoB: 25 March 2000 **Place of Birth:** London
England Debut: 12 October 2018 v Croatia (A)

Jadon made three appearances for England at UEFA Euro 2020, bringing his caps total to 22 by the end of the tournament. His first international goals came as he bagged a brace in a 5-3 victory over Kosovo at Southampton's St Mary's Stadium in September 2019 while he was also on target in a 3-0 win against the Republic of Ireland in November 2020. Previously capped between U16 and U19 level, the forward was part of England's U17s squad that won the 2017 FIFA U17 World Cup.

DOMINIC CALVERT-LEWIN

Position: Forward
DoB: 16 March 1997 **Place of Birth:** Sheffield
England Debut: 8 October 2020 v Wales (H)

Dominic scored four times for England during the 2020/21 season, with a debut strike against Wales in a 3-0 win, a goal in a 3-0 success against Republic of Ireland and a brace in a 5-0 home triumph over San Marino. He made the Three Lions squad for UEFA Euro 2020, appearing in two matches at the competition as a substitute. The forward previously appeared for the Young Lions at U20 and U21 level and scored the winning goal as they beat Venezuela 1-0 in the final of the 2017 FIFA U-20 World Cup.

ENGLAND TIMELINE

A Brief Plotted History of the England Women's Team

1972

England's women's senior team beat Scotland 3-2 in Greenock in their first-ever international on 18 November 1972.

1987

England once again qualified for the four-team European Competition for Women's Football tournament in 1987. Unfortunately, this time they were beaten 3-2 after extra-time in the semi-finals by Sweden in Moss, Norway.

1993

In 1993, the Football Association took over the running of the women's game in England. Two years later, the Lionesses qualified for the UEFA Women's European Championships, having missed out on the previous three editions.

UEFA Competition For National Representative Women's Teams

FINAL 2nd LEG

Sunday, 27th May, 1984
KICK-OFF 2.30 p.m.

ENGLAND v SWEDEN

Luton Town F.C.,
Kenilworth Road, Luton.

1984

The Lionesses reached the final of the inaugural UEFA European Competition for Representative Women's Teams with a 3-1 aggregate victory over Denmark in April 1984. The following month Martin Reagan's team were beaten 4-3 on penalties by Sweden in the final after a 1-1 aggregate draw.

1998

Hope Powell became England's first full-time coach in June 1998. During her 15-year reign, Powell guided the Lionesses to the 2001, 2005, 2009 and 2013 editions of the UEFA Women's Championship and the FIFA Women's World Cup in 2007 and 2011. In 2003, Powell became the first woman to obtain football's top coaching qualification: the UEFA Pro Licence.

2009

One of England's biggest achievements under Powell's management was a run to the Final of the UEFA Women's European Championships in 2009. With a 3-2 victory over Russia and a 1-1 draw with Sweden, the Lionesses advanced to the knockout phase as one of the competition's best third-place teams. They beat Finland and the Netherlands to reach the Final, before going down to a heavy defeat to Germany.

2012

Many of England's top players, including current Lionesses Karen Bardsley, Steph Houghton, Jill Scott and Ellen White, were included in Great Britain's squad for the 2012 Olympic Games.

2015

England's best showing at a FIFA Women's World Cup came in 2015, as the Lionesses finished third at the tournament. Mark Sampson's side won two of their three Group F fixtures to progress to the knockout phase. Victories over Norway and Canada took England to the semi-finals, where they were beaten 2-1 by Japan. A 1-0 extra-time win over Germany saw Sampson's team come out on top in the third-place play-off.

2019

England once again progressed to the semi-final of the FIFA Women's World Cup in France in 2019. Three wins out of three saw them top Group D, while a 3-0 win over Cameroon saw them make the quarter-finals, where they beat Norway by the same score line. A 2-1 defeat to the United States in the semi-finals was followed by a 2-1 loss to Sweden in the third-place play-off. Later that year, the Lionesses welcomed a record crowd for a home international as 77,768 fans saw them take on Germany at Wembley Stadium.

WOMEN'S SENIOR TEAM: CHART TOPPERS

Here's a list of the Top All-Time Appearance Makers and Goal Scorers.

TOP ALL-TIME APPEARANCE MAKERS

RANKING: 1st

PLAYER: FARA WILLIAMS MBE
SENIOR ENGLAND CAREER: 2001-2019
CAPS: 172 GOALS: 40

Fara Williams announced her retirement from playing in April 2021, bringing down the curtain on a remarkable career that saw her win four club major trophies with the likes of Everton, Liverpool and Arsenal while she collected an MBE (Member of the Order of the British Empire) in the 2016 New Years Honours list. Having made her senior England debut against Portugal in November 2001, Williams went on to become the Lionesses most capped player of all time, making a total of 172 international appearances.

RANKING: 2nd

PLAYER: JILL SCOTT MBE
SENIOR ENGLAND CAREER: 2006-to date
CAPS: 151 GOALS: 25

With over 150 caps to her name, Sunderland-born Jill Scott continues to be an important component in England's midfield. Scott's Lionesses debut came against the Netherlands in August 2006. Since then, the 2016 FA WSL winner has been selected for England squads for the 2007, 2011, 2015 and 2019 FIFA Women's World Cups and the UEFA Women's European Championships in 2009, 2013 and 2017.

RANKING: 3rd

PLAYER: KAREN CARNEY MBE
SENIOR ENGLAND CAREER: 2005-2019
CAPS: 144 GOALS: 32

Karen Carney was just 14 years old when she made her senior club debut for Birmingham City against Fulham in 2001. Four years later, the two-time FA Young Player of the Year came off the bench to score in a 4-1 win over Italy in her first England appearance. The midfield creator, known as the 'wizard', was a prolific trophy winner during her career with eleven major honours in the English club game alone. She also won three Cyprus Cups and the SheBelieves Cup during her 14-year-long international stint.

RANKING: 4th

PLAYER: ALEX SCOTT MBE
SENIOR ENGLAND CAREER: 2004-2017
CAPS: 140 GOALS: 12

Best known these days as the presenter of the BBC show, Football Focus, Alex Scott's football career began when she started training with Arsenal aged eight. She rose through the ranks to become a Gunners regular in two spells with the club for whom she won five top-flight titles and seven FA Women's Cups. Between 2004 and 2017, she established herself as England's first-choice right-back and travelled with the Lionesses to four UEFA Women's European Championships and three FIFA Women's World Cups.

RANKING: 5th

PLAYER: CASEY STONEY MBE
SENIOR ENGLAND CAREER: 2000-2018
CAPS: 130 GOALS: 6

A versatile defender, Casey Stoney was twice named England Women's Player of the Year during distinguished career for the Lionesses. The Basildon-born player first featured for her country as a substitute in a match against France in August 2000, while she was called up to the squad for four UEFA Women's European Championships and three FIFA Women's World Cups.

TOP ALL-TIME GOAL SCORERS

RANKING: 1st

PLAYER: KELLY SMITH MBE
SENIOR ENGLAND CAREER: 1995-2014
GOALS: 46 CAPS: 117

Kelly Smith debuted for England against Italy in November 1995, just three days after celebrating her 17th birthday. Her first international goal came on the occasion of her second cap, against Croatia later that month. Smith became England's all-time leading goal scorer in February 2012 as her brace against Finland took her to tally to 45 strikes for her country. Her final goal for England came in a 4-4 draw with Scotland at the 2013 Cyprus Cup.

RANKING: 2nd

PLAYER: KERRY DAVIS
SENIOR ENGLAND CAREER: 1982-1998
GOALS: 44 CAPS: 82

There is some uncertainty over Kerry Davis' record as the Lionesses' second most prolific goal scorer, as it isn't known how many of her 44 strikes came in 'official' fixtures. What isn't in any doubt is the impact the Stoke-on-Trent born forward made wearing an England shirt. She helped her country to reach the semi-final stage of the 1987 UEFA Women's European Championships and the quarter-finals of the 1995 FIFA Women's World Cup.

RANKING: JOINT 3rd

PLAYER: KAREN WALKER
SENIOR ENGLAND CAREER: 1988-2003
GOALS: 40 CAPS: 83

With some dispute over Kerry Davis' tally, Karen Walker was once considered England's record goal scorer, with 40 strikes in 83 appearances. The former Doncaster Rovers Belles and Leeds United player made her Lionesses' debut as a teenager back in July 1988 against an Italy 'B' team in the Mundialito tournament. Her uncompromised playing style earned her the nickname 'Wacker' during her career.

RANKING: JOINT 3d

PLAYER: FARA WILLIAMS MBE
SENIOR ENGLAND CAREER: 2001-2019
GOALS: 40 CAPS: 172

Fara Williams, England's most capped player, also ranks high on the Lionesses' all-time goal scoring list. The London-born midfielder opened her international account with a strike a 3-0 win over Portugal in a 2003 FIFA Women's World Cup qualifier in Portsmouth back in February 2002. She followed that up with 39 further goals, including a hat-trick in an 8-0 thrashing of Malta in Blackpool in October 2009.

RANKING: 5th

PLAYER: ELLEN WHITE
SENIOR ENGLAND CAREER: 2010-to date
GOALS: 39 CAPS: 95

Two-time England Player of the Year Ellen White was just seven strikes off becoming the Lionesses all-time record goal scorer at the time of writing. The Aylesbury forward opened her England goals account in the 3-0 win over Austria at Loftus Road back in March 2010. Her six strikes at the 2019 FIFA Women's World Cup helped take her country to the semi-finals of the tournament, while she collected the Bronze boot in the process.

THE LIONESSES' HEAD COACH:
SARINA WIEGMAN

Name: Sarina Wiegman
Date of Birth: 26 October 1969
Place of Birth: The Hague,
Netherlands

A standout player from an early age, Sarina Wiegman earned her first senior Netherlands call-up at just 16 years of age. By the time she was 17, she had helped her club side Kruikelientjes '71 win the Dutch Cup.

Playing at an international tournament in China in 1988, she bumped into the US national team manager Anson Dorrance. He invited Wiegman to play for the North Carolina Tar Heels. Wiegman packed her bags and spent a year there. During her time in America, the Dutch international won the league title and got to play with some of the States's biggest stars, including Kristine Lilly, Carla Overbeck and Mia Hamm.

When she returned to Holland, Wiegman had to find a part-time job which could financially support her footballing exploits. This was the situation for all Dutch female footballers at the time. She became a PE teacher at a local school, a job she kept throughout her nine-year stay at club side Ter Leede.

The defensive midfielder earned two league titles and one cup while at Ter Leede, eventually hanging up her boots in 2003, one year after she had earned the final of 104 caps for the Dutch national team. She had become the first Dutch player - male or female - to reach a century of international caps.

Wiegman first ventured into management in 2006, leading her former side Ter Leede to a league and cup double - their first silverware for three years. After a memorable debut season as a manager, she left for ADO Den Haag. In a seven-year spell at the club based in the Hague, she lifted one league trophy and two domestic cups.

She then moved to the Netherlands national team's management staff, where she spent three years as assistant manager first to Roger Reijners and then to Arjan van der Laan, with a short spell as interim manager in between. In October 2016, she simultaneously became assistant manager of the Sparta Rotterdam men's youth team and became the first woman to coach in the professional men's game in Holland in the process.

Just before Christmas of the same year, she became Netherlands interim boss for the second time. She was ultimately handed the job on a permanent basis the following month. Despite poor form in pre-tournament friendlies and with only six months to go until a European Championship, Wiegman led the Dutch to a stunning title win at UEFA Women's Euro 2017. Her side won every match, including victories over Norway, Sweden and England. She won FIFA Women's Coach of the Year as a result.

In 2019, Wiegman led the Dutch to the World Cup final, although they were beaten by eventual champions the United States. She took over as England manager having taken charge of the Netherlands at the rescheduled Tokyo Olympics in the summer of 2021.

LIONESSES UNDER HEGE RIISE

In between the departure of Phil Neville and the arrival of Sarina Wiegman, Norwegian Hege Riise took temporary charge of the Lionesses.

Netherlands boss Sarina Wiegman was due to succeed Phil Neville as England women's team Head Coach after the delayed Tokyo Olympics in the summer of 2021. But when Neville departed the role early in January 2021, to become manager of David Beckham's MLS side Inter Miami, the Lionesses needed an Interim Coach…

Step forward, Hege Riise.

With an Olympic gold medal and 188 caps for Norway to her name, scarcely could England have called on someone with more pedigree on the international stage. And what a first match she was to experience in the Lionesses' hotseat. Her side romped to a 6-0 victory over an in-form Northern Ireland in February 2021 in England's first game in almost a year. Ellen White, so often Neville's talesman during his three years in charge of England, got her first international hat-trick that afternoon at St George's Park.

Other experienced heads like Lucy Bronze and Rachel Daly got on the scoresheet while Jill Scott earned her 150th cap. Riise also used the game to introduce some promising youngsters who had shone in the FA Women's Super League in the 11 months since England were last in action. Lotte Wubben-Moy and Ebony Salmon made confident debuts, as did goalkeeper Sandy MacIver. Another debutant, Ella Toone, was handed the chance to score from the penalty spot late-on. She calmy slotted the ball into the corner from 12 yards to round off the 6-0 triumph.

April 2021 saw a double-header for Lionesses against France and Canada. France dominated proceedings at the Stade Michel d'Ornano in Caen and without injured captain Steph Houghton, England went down to a 3-1 defeat. Fran Kirby's late penalty proved to be nothing more than a consolation for Riise's side with Sandy Baltimore, Viviane Asseyi and Marie Katoto on target for the hosts.

A few days later, a defensive mix-up allowed Canada to take a third-minute lead at Stoke's bet365 Stadium through Évelyne Viens. England settled and started to test their opponents' defence thereafter but their opponents doubled their advantage four minutes from time when Nichelle Prince beat Karen Bardsley to the ball to slide it over the goal line.

After her spell as England Interim Coach, Riise got to work with a number of Lionesses during the summer of 2021 as manager of Team GB's women's football team for the delayed 2020 Toyko Olympics.

29

ENGLAND WOMEN'S SENIOR TEAM

(H) Home (A) Away (N) Neutral Venue

KAREN BARDSLEY

Position: Goalkeeper
DoB: 14 October 1984   Place of Birth: Santa Monica, United States
England Debut: 09 March 2005 v Northern Ireland (N)

A stalwart for England, Karen has won over 80 caps since 2005. The United States-born goalkeeper chose to represent the Lionesses owing to her family connections in Stockport. She was included in the England squad for the 2011, 2015 and 2019 FIFA Women's World Cups. She was also part of the group that finished as runners-up at the 2009 UEFA Women's European Championships and travelled with the Lionesses to the 2013 and 2017 tournaments.

CARLY TELFORD

Position: Goalkeeper
DoB: 07 July 1987   Place of Birth: Newcastle
England Debut: 11 March 2007 v Scotland (H)

Having previously been an unused substitute at the 2007 and 2015 FIFA Women's World Cups and well as UEFA Women's Euro 2017, Carly made her baptism at a major tournament with three appearances at the 2019 FIFA Women's World Cup. The former Sunderland, Leeds and Perth Glory (loan) goalkeeper was in her third spell at Chelsea at the time of writing (ahead of the start of the 2021/22 FA WSL season). She has over 20 senior caps to her name, having previously represented England at U17, U19, U21 and U23 level.

MARY EARPS

Position: Goalkeeper
DoB: 07 March 1993   Place of Birth: Nottingham
England Debut: 11 June 2017 v Switzerland (A)

During her time at Loughborough University, Mary was part of the same Great Britain squad as Isobel Christiansen, Fran Kirby, Kerys Harrop and Demi Stokes that won gold at the 2013 Summer Universiade. Having represented England at U17, U19 and U23 level, the goalkeeper had made eight senior appearances for the Lionesses at the time of writing (prior to the 2023 FIFA Women's World Cup qualifier against North Macedonia in September 2021). At club level, she moved from VfL Wolfsburg to Manchester United in 2019.

ELLIE ROEBUCK

Position: Goalkeeper
DoB: 23 September 1999   Place of Birth: Sheffield
England Debut: 08 November 2018 v Austria (A)

Ellie has impressed for both club and country since making her FA WSL debut for Manchester City in 2018. The former Sheffield United's Centre of Excellence attendee was part of the Young Lionesses team that finished third at the 2018 FIFA U20 Women's World Cup while she had made her senior international debut by the end of that year. She was one of two Lionesses goalkeepers selected to appear for the Team GB squad for the delayed 2020 Olympic Games along with Carly Telford.

SANDY MACIVER

Position: Goalkeeper
DoB: 18 June 1998   Place of Birth: Winsford
England Debut: 23 February 2021 v Northern Ireland (H)

Signed by Everton in 2020, Sandy was named Player of the Match in that year's Women's FA Cup Final, despite being on the losing side again Manchester City – the club the goalkeeper trained with as a youngster. Sandy has represented England at U17, U19, U20 and U21 and was part of the squad that finished third at the 2018 FIFA U20 Women's World Cup where she was awarded the Golden Glove as the tournament's best goalkeeper.

HANNAH HAMPTON
Position: Goalkeeper
DoB: 16 November 2000   Place of Birth: Birmingham
England Debut: -

Born in Birmingham but raised in Spain from the age of five, Hannah trained with Villarreal CF as a youngster. She moved back to England in 2010, joining Stoke City's academy before making her senior debut for Birmingham City in 2017. Capped by England at all levels between U15 and U21 level, Hannah received her first senior call-up as a member of the Lionesses travelling party for the 2020 SheBelieves Cup. She signed for Aston Villa in the summer of 2021.

LUCY BRONZE
Position: Defender
DoB: 28 October 1991   Place of Birth: Berwick-upon-Tweed
England Debut: 26 June 2013 v Japan (H)

One of the standout performers of the women's game, Lucy has twice won the PFA Women's Players' Player of the Year award (2014 and 2017) and the BBC Women's Footballer of the Year award (2018 and 2020) while she collected the Silver Ball after her showings at the 2019 FIFA Women's World Cup. She is also the first Lioness to be named in the top three nominees for the Ballon d'Or Féminin, as she finished second place in the prestigious award in 2019. A mainstay of the England squad since 2013, the defender has over 80 caps to her name to date.

ALEX GREENWOOD
Position: Defender
DoB: 07 September 1993   Place of Birth: Liverpool
England Debut: 05 March 2014 v Italy (N)

Having joined Manchester City from Olympique Lyonnais in 2020, Alex won the Women's FA Cup in her debut year with the Citizens. Having previously appeared for England at the 2015 FIFA Women's World Cup, she was one of the stars of the 2019 tournament, where she featured in four matches and score a memorable goal against Cameroon in the round of 16. She also was a key member of the Lioness squad that reached the semi-finals of UEFA Women's Euro 2017.

STEPH HOUGHTON
Position: Defender
DoB: 23 April 1988   Place of Birth: Durham
England Debut: March 8, 2007 v Russia (H)

England's 'Captain Marvel', Steph has over 120 caps to her name. Having suffered the disappointment of missing the 2007 FIFA Women's World Cup and UEFA Women's Euro 2009 through injury, the defender has featured at every major tournament for the Lionesses since. She captained England to third and fourth place finishes at the 2015 and 2019 FIFA Women's World Cups respectively, as well as the skippering the side which reached the semi-finals of UEFA Women's Euro 2017.

MILLIE BRIGHT
Position: Defender
DoB: 21 August 1993   Place of Birth: Chesterfield
England Debut: 20 September 2016 v Belgium (A)

A regular for England, Millie was the only Lioness to feature at every match at UEFA Women's Euro 2017, despite having made her senior international debut only 10 months earlier. Two years later, the Chelsea player featured in five of the Lionesses' seven matches at the 2019 FIFA Women's World Cup and, at the time of writing, had won 39 senior caps. In the summer of 2021, she was included in the Team GB squad for the delayed Tokyo Olympic Games.

DEMI STOKES
Position: Defender
DoB: 12 December 1991   Place of Birth: Dudley
England Debut: 17 January 2014 v Norway (N)

By the end of the 2020/21 season, Demi had won six major trophies with her club side Manchester City. At international level, she represented England at U19, U20 and U23 level prior to her inclusion in a 30-player senior squad for a training camp in La Manga, Spain in 2014 during which time she made her Lionesses debut in a 1-1 friendly draw with Norway. The defender has won over 50 caps to date, with her one and only international goal at the time of writing having come in a 9-0 victory over Montenegro in a 2015 FIFA Women's World Cup qualifier in Brighton in April 2014.

LEAH WILLIAMSON
Position: Defender
DoB: 29 March 1997 Place of Birth: Milton Keynes
England Debut: 08 June 2018 v Russia (A)

Arsenal through-and-through, Leah signed a new contract with her beloved club in the summer of 2021 prior to representing Team GB at the Olympics. The defender's passion for the Gunners is replicated in her love for England, for whom she has won over 20 caps. She was named in the Lionesses squad for the 2019 FIFA Women's World Cup, which saw her make her tournament debut as a substitute against Cameroon. That same year, she scored her first international goal: an 86th-minute winner in in a 3–2 friendly triumph over the Czech Republic in November 2019.

ABBIE MCMANUS
Position: Defender
DoB: 14 January 1993 Place of Birth: Prestwich
England Debut: 01 March 2018 v France (N)

Abbie had played almost 20 matches for England at the time of writing, which included three appearances (two starts) at the 2019 FIFA Women's World Cup. She also featured in two of the three games at the 2019 SheBelieves Cup, which saw the Lionesses win the competition. At club level, Abbie signed for Manchester United from rivals Manchester City in 2019 and was loaned to Tottenham Hotspur in 2021.

RACHEL DALY
Position: Defender/Forward
DoB: 06 December 1991 Place of Birth: Harrogate
England Debut: 04 June 2016 v Serbia (H)

After turning out for England at various levels between U15 and U23, Rachel scored on her senior debut in a 7-0 victory over Serbia in a UEFA Women's Euro 2017 qualifier. She has since won over 35 caps for Lionesses with her goal in the 6-0 win over Northern Ireland in February 2021 her marking her fourth senior international strike. Plying her trade for National Women's Soccer League (NWSL) side Houston Dash at the time of writing, the versatile player – who can operate in defence or attack – was loaned to FA WSL team West Ham United in 2020.

LOTTE WUBBEN-MOY
Position: Defender
DoB: 11 January 1999 Place of Birth: London
England Debut: 23 February 2021 v Northern Ireland (H)

Lotte came on as a substitute for Arsenal teammate Leah Williamson in England's 6-0 triumph over Northern Ireland in February 2021 at St George's Park. The defender, who captained England U17s at the 2016 FIFA U17 Women's World Cup has had two spells with the Gunners to date in between a spell playing college soccer for Atlantic Coast Conference (ACC) side North Carolina Tar Heels in the United States.

MIDFIELDERS

KEIRA WALSH
Position: Midfielder
DoB: 08 April 1997 Place of Birth: Rochdale
England Debut: 28 November 2017 v Kazakhstan (H)

Less than 12 months on from making her senior debut, Keira captained the Lionesses for the first time in a 6-0 win over Kazakhstan in September 2018. The midfielder appeared in all three of England's matches as the won the SheBelieves Cup in 2019 and featured in five matches at the FIFA Women's World Cup that same year. She signed a new, three-year contract with Manchester City in 2020, for whom she has won seven major trophies to date.

JILL SCOTT

Position: Midfielder
DoB: 02 February 1987 Place of Birth: Sunderland
England Debut: 31 August 2006 v Netherlands (H)

Jill continues move towards Fara Williams' all-time appearance record for England. The midfielder has 151 caps for the Lionesses at the time of writing, while Williams' tally stands at 172. One of just 11 Lionesses centurions, Jill has been selected in the squad for seven major tournaments to date: the FIFA Women's World Cup in 2007, 2011, 2015 and 2019 as well as the UEFA Women's European Championships in 2009, 2013 and 2017.

JADE MOORE

Position: Midfielder
DoB: 22 October 1990 Place of Birth: Worksop
England Debut: 28 February 2012 v Finland (N)

A former U19, U20 and U23 international, Jade was included in the Lionesses' squads for the 2013 and 2017 UEFA Women's European Championships and the 2015 and 2019 FIFA Women's World Cups. She played in four matches at the latter tournament, with her start against Sweden in the third-place play-off marking her 50th senior appearance for England. Her only international goal to date came against Italy in the 2012 Cyprus Cup.

GEORGIA STANWAY

Position: Midfielder
DoB: 03 January 1999 Place of Birth: Barrow-in-Furness
England Debut: 08 November 2018 v Austria (A)

Previously capped at U15, U17, U19 and U20 level, Georgia was the joint top-goal scorer at the 2018 FIFA U20 World Cup in France with six strikes. She was one of two players, along with Chioma Ubogagu, to net on her senior England debut in a 3-0 win over Austria in November 2018. On the back of being named the PFA Women's Young Player of the Year in 2018/19, Georgia was the youngest player to be included in Phil Neville's squad for the 2019 FIFA Women's World Cup, aged 20 at the time. She went on to feature in five matches at the tournament.

LUCY STANIFORTH

Position: Midfielder
DoB: 02 October 1992 Place of Birth: York
England Debut: 04 September 2018 v Kazakhstan (A)

Lucy helped England to victory at the 2019 SheBelieves Cup, scoring the opening goal in a 3-0 win over Japan at the tournament. She also appeared at the 2020 competition, coming on as a second-half substitute for Georgia Stanway in the 1-0 triumph over Japan. The midfielder, who signed for Manchester United in July 2020, has made over 15 appearances for England to date having previously featured at U17, U19, U20 and U23 level. She was included in the 23-player squad for the 2019 FIFA Women's World Cup.

JORDAN NOBBS

Position: Midfielder
DoB: 08 December 1992 Place of Birth: Stockton-on-Tees
England Debut: 06 March 2013 v Italy (N)

Jordan's promise as a young player was emphasised when she was called into the England U15 squad at the age of 12 and captained the side against Wales at 13. Also capped at U17, U19, U20 and U23 level, her senior Lionesses debut came at the age of 19. Having appeared for the Lionesses at the 2013 and 2017 UEFA Women's Championships and the 2015 FIFA Women's World Cup, the Arsenal player suffered the heartbreak of missing out on the 2019 FIFA Women's World Cup with a knee injury. She returned to the Lionesses' line-up in late 2019 and appeared in all three games at the 2020 SheBelieves Cup.

NIAMH CHARLES

Position: Midfielder
DoB: 21 June 1999   Place of Birth: Wirral
England Debut: 09 April 2021 v France (A)

The last couple of years have been pretty eventful for Niamh, who moved from her childhood club Liverpool to join reigning FA WSL Champions Chelsea in 2020. Having been an impressive performer for the Young Lions – helping the U17s finish third at the UEFA Women's U17 Championship and reach the quarter-finals of the FIFA U17 World Cup in 2016 – the defender came on as a half-time substitute for Alex Greenwood to make her senior Lionesses debut against France in April 2021.

NIKITA PARRIS

Position: Forward
DoB: 10 March 1994   Place of Birth: Toxteth
England Debut: 04 June 2016 v Serbia (H)

Nikita got England's memorable 2019 FIFA Women's World Cup campaign underway by slotting home a penalty in the 2-1 win over Scotland in opening Group D fixture in Nice. The forward, who is the sister of professional boxer Natasha Jonas, is no stranger to scoring important goals for the Lionesses having got the winner against Portugal at UEFA Women's Euro 2017 and a strike against the United States in the successful 2019 SheBelieves Cup campaign. The Arsenal player won her 50th England cap in the 1-0 SheBelieves Cup defeat to Spain in March 2020.

FRAN KIRBY

Position: Forward
DoB: 29 June 1993   Place of Birth: Reading
England Debut: 03 August 2014 v Sweden (H)

After a limited number of appearances during the 2019/20 season due to injury and illness, Fran bounced back in 2020/21 to win both the PFA Women's Players' Player of the Year and FAW Women's Footballer of the Year awards. She had previously won both awards in 2017/18. Fran scored on her return to England action, after a near two-year absence, slotting home a penalty in the 3-1 defeat to France in April 2021. It was her 13th goal in 44 senior England matches at that point.

TONI DUGGAN

Position: Forward
DoB: 25 July 1991   Place of Birth: Liverpool
England Debut: 19 September 2012 v Croatia (H)

Toni was a key member of Mo Marley's Young Lionesses squad that won the UEFA Women's U19 Championship back in 2009. The forward scored four goals as England won the competition for the first time. Toni was also capped at U17, U20 and U23 level as a youngster prior to making her senior debut in a 3-0 win over Croatia in September 2012. She has made over 75 international appearances since then and scored many important goals for her country, including hat-tricks against Turkey in September 2013 and Montenegro in April 2014.

ELLEN WHITE

Position: Forward
DoB: 09 May 1989   Place of Birth: Aylesbury
England Debut: 25 March 2010 v Austria (H)

Ellen's hat-trick in the 6-0 win over Northern Ireland in February 2021 took her goal tally for England to 39 – seven strikes short of equalling Kelly Smith's all-time goal scoring record for the Lionesses. Just over a year after making her senior international debut in 2010, the striker announced herself on the global stage, with an incredible lob against eventual tournament winners Japan at the 2011 FIFA Women's World Cup. The two-time England Senior Women's Player of the Year has since appeared at two further World Cups, which saw her country finish third at the 2015 competition while she won the Bronze Boot in 2019 as they reached the semi-finals.

BETH MEAD

Position: Forward
DoB: 09 May 1995 Place of Birth: Whitby
England Debut: 06 April 2018 v Wales (H)

Arsenal striker Beth played a crucial role in England's SheBelieves Cup success in 2019 as she netted in victories over Brazil and Japan. She was also in fine form at that summer's FIFA Women's World Cup, setting up three goals for her teammates during the tournament. The 2016 PFA Women's Young Player of the Year scored her eighth goal for her country in a 3-2 victory over Czech Republic in November 2019.

BETHANY ENGLAND

Position: Forward
DoB: 03 June 1994 Place of Birth: Barnsley
England Debut: 29 August 2019 v Belgium (A)

With the perfect surname for a Lioness, Bethany represented her country at U19 and U23 level prior to her first senior call-up for England's back-to-back fixtures with Belgium and Norway in August 2019. Her first international goal came in a 2-1 defeat to Brazil at Middlesbrough's Riverside Stadium in October 2019 while she was on target a month later in a 3-2 triumph in the Czech Republic. The forward has won numerous trophies at club level during her career, including the FA WSL with Chelsea in 2017/18 and 2019/20.

LAUREN HEMP

Position: Forward
DoB: 07 August 2000 Place of Birth: North Walsham
England Debut: 8 October 2019 v Portugal (A)

After winning eight caps for England, Lauren was included in the Team GB squad for the delayed Olympic Games in the summer of 2021. The three-time PFA Women's Young Player of the Year, who celebrated her 21st birthday in August 2021, has already achieved a great deal in her fledgling career. She helped the Young Lionesses finish third at the FIFA U20 Women's World Cup in 2018, the same year she signed for FA WSL powerhouse Manchester City, with her senior Lionesses debut following in 2019.

CHLOE KELLY

Position: Forward
DoB: 15 January 1998 Place of Birth: London
England Debut: 8 November 2018 v Austria (A)

Having started her senior career at Arsenal, Chloe made a real name for herself at Everton, where she was named in the PFA FA WSL Team of the Year in 2020 – the same year she moved to Manchester City. Two years after making her Lionesses' debut, the forward featured in matches against USA and Spain at the 2020 SheBelieves Cup. At the time of writing, she had won seven senior caps for England with plenty more surely to follow.

ELLA TOONE

Position: Forward
DoB: 02 September 1999 Place of Birth: Tyldesley
England Debut: 23 February 2021 v Northern Ireland (H)

Ella was one of four Lionesses to make their England debut against Northern Ireland in February 2021. She came on as a half-time substitute for Jordan Nobbs in the match and got her first international goal just 29 minutes later, slotting home a penalty. Having previously represented Blackburn Rovers and Manchester City, the former England U17, U19 and U21 player signed for Manchester United in 2018.

GUESS THE GOAL SCORER

Can you identify these England goal scorers from the photographs and clues?!

A) "I gave England an early lead in our 2018 FIFA World Cup semi-final against Croatia with a curling free-kick. Who am I?"

B) "I scored England's opening goal at the 2019 FIFA Women's World Cup from the penalty spot. Who am I?"

C) "I came off the bench to make my senior England debut against Lithuania in March 2015 and headed home my first international goal just 80 seconds later. Who am I?"

D) "I marked my inclusion in my first senior England squad for a major competition by scoring an audacious lob against eventual tournament winners Japan at the 2011 FIFA Women's World Cup. Who am I?"

E) "An unlikely goal scorer – I netted in a penalty shootout (and saved a penalty too!) as we beat Switzerland 6-5 on spot kicks in the 2019 UEFA Nations League finals match for third place in. Who am I?"

F) "I was one of two debutants, along with Chioma Ubogagu, to score on my Lionesses' debut in a 3-0 away win in Austria in November 2018. Who am I?"

G) "I gave England the lead in their 6-1 thrashing of Panama at the 2018 FIFA World Cup and I scored again before half-time. Who am I?"

H) "I'm a defender by trade but I scored a match-winning goal – my first for the Lionesses – in the 86th-minute of a 3–2 friendly victory over the Czech Republic in November 2019. Who am I?"

Answers on pages 60-61

SURVIVE. REVIVE. THRIVE.

The Football Association has an ambitious strategy in place for grassroots football.

On the back of the challenges presented by the COVID-19 pandemic, the FA launched a new strategy in 2021 for grassroots football in England, which provides clear direction for the many millions that play nationwide

The strategy - Survive. Revive. Thrive. - has seven transformational objectives focusing on:

- **Male Participation:** Modernised opportunities to retain and re-engage millions of male participants in the game.

- **Female Participation:** A sustainable model based on a world-class, modernised offer.

- **Club Network:** A vibrant national club network that delivers inclusive, safe local grassroots football and meets community needs.

- **Facilities:** Enhanced access to good quality pitches across grassroots football.

- **Grassroots Workforce:** A transformation in community football by inspiring, supporting and retaining volunteers in the game.

- **Digital Products and Services:** An efficient grassroots digital ecosystem to serve the administrative and development needs of players, parents and the workforce.

- **Positive Environment:** A game that's representative of our diverse footballing communities, played in a safe and inclusive environment.

The four-season long strategy came into effect on 29 March 2021 when grassroots football returned after a COVID-19 lockdown. The immediate vision was to get grassroots football back on its feet after year of unprecedented difficulties.

The new strategy set out a number of goals to revive the game by addressing the areas that require particular attention. This includes increasing opportunities to ensure girls have the same access as boys to football in schools and clubs, and improving quality of pitches, with the aim of seeing 5000 good-quality pitches added to the current number by 2024.

The strategy looks ahead to ensure the game can thrive in the future. Not only encouraging new participation at every age group and from historically under-represented groups, but also harnessing the power of digital to better connect participants to the game they love. It also means ensuring the game is played in a safe, welcoming and inclusive environment.

Underpinning the strategy is the long-standing partnership between the FA and County FAs, which will be crucial to its success. The partnership is committed to serving those that participate and are involved in the game, and providing the leadership needed to ensure future generations benefit from it as much as those that have played before.

Both the FA and County FAs are not-for-profit organisations that reinvest all of the money that they make back into football and they are planning to invest over £180m into grassroots football over the four seasons of the strategy.

Speaking after the launch of the strategy, the FA's director of football development, James Kendall, commented; "We're delighted to see the safe return of the grassroots game and are excited to announce our new four-year strategy after what has been an extremely difficult year.

"Our commitment to grassroots football has remained resolute and this strategy is a clear demonstration of our long-term ambitions, which will ultimately play a role in improving the health and wellbeing of millions of individuals across the nation.

"This new strategy aims to ensure the grassroots game in England will survive, revive and thrive over the next four years.

"I'm confident that we'll seize on the remarkable togetherness and resilience our national game has shown in the face of COVID-19 and use it as a force for good. We recognise there's a huge amount to achieve, but we have set ourselves the challenge and look forward to delivering on this strategy which puts players at the very heart of everything we do."

Whether your interest in taking part in grassroots football lies in playing, coaching or refereeing, you can find out more at www.thefa.com/get-involved

SPOT THE DIFFERENCE

Can you spot the ten differences between these two pictures of when England took on Denmark to win 2-1 in the UEFA Euro semi-final?

THE GOAL SCORING TRAIL

Harry Kane, Phil Foden and Marcus Rashford are all practising their shots at goal. Can you guess who is going to score?

ENGLAND QUIZ

Put your knowledge of the Three Lions and Lionesses' to the test.

1 Which stadium will host England's first Group A match at UEFA Women's Euro 2022?

2 Who did England play in their UEFA Euro 2020 round of 16 match?

3 Who was the manager of England when they won the FIFA World Cup in 1966?

4 Which city were Harry Maguire and Ellie Roebuck born in?

5 What year did the Lionesses complete their best showing at a FIFA Women's World Cup to date, finishing third at the tournament?

6 Who scored two penalties for England in a 3-2 extra-time victory over Cameroon in a FIFA World Cup quarter-final tie in 1990?

7 How many nations will compete in the 2022 FIFA World Cup?

8 ...and how many will compete in the 2026 tournament?

9 Can you name the three club sides England Head Coach Gareth Southgate used to play for?

10 Who took temporary charge of the Lionesses following the departure of Phil Neville and the arrival of current Head Coach Sarina Wiegman?

11 Which former Lioness is the only player to appear in England women's top five goal scoring and appearance making lists?

12 Which Lioness was second in Ballon d'Or Feminin and won the FIFA Women's World Cup Silver Ball award in 2019?

13 Who did the Three Lions thrash 4-1 at UEFA Euro 1996?

14 Which former Wales international is currently the Three Lions' main Goalkeeping Coach?

15 Who is the Three Lions' top all-time goal scorer?

16 Which current England defender started his career representing the likes of Yate Town and Chippenham Town?

17 Which current England player became the Three Lions' third-youngest debutant of all time when he came on as a substitute for Mason Mouth in the in the 3-0 win over the Republic of Ireland in November 2020?

18 How many goals did Harry Kane score at the 2018 FIFA World Cup to win the tournament's Golden Boot?

19 What is the name of the Swedish manager who took charge of England in the 2002 and 2006 FIFA World Cups?

20 What was the name of the black and white mongrel dog who found the Jules Rimet Trophy (FIFA World Cup) when it went missing in 1966?!

21 Who were the opponents for both England men's and women's first ever international match?

22 What order of chivalry have past and present Lionesses such as Fara Williams, Jill Scott, Karen Carney, Alex Scott and Casey Stoney all been presented with?

23 Who is the Lionesses' top all-time goal scorer?

24 Which Lioness scored six goals at the 2019 FIFA Women's World Cup to claim the tournament's Bronze Boot?

25 Who scored his first international hat-trick in the 5-0 win over the Czech Republic in March 2019?

26 Who became the first full-time Head Coach of the Lionesses back in June 1998?

27 Which major sporting event did Lionesses such as Ellie Roebuck, Leah Williamson, Jill Scott and Fran Kirby compete in Japan in the summer of 2021?

28 What tournament did the Three Lions appear in for the first time in 1950?

29 ...And what competition did they first appear in 1968?

30 What nationality is the Lionesses' Head Coach, Sarina Wiegman?

Answers on pages 60-61.

BEHIND THE SCENES

St. George's Park was the Three Lions' base during UEFA Euro 2020.

Gareth Southgate's England squad arrived at the familiar surroundings of St. George's Park (SGP) on Tuesday 8 June 2021 ahead of the start of the delayed UEFA Euro 2020 tournament, which kicked-off three days later. The 330-acre facility is where the Three Lions are usually based prior to international matches, so it was very much a 'home-from-home' for Southgate's men during the competition.

Speaking of home, the on-site 228-bed Hilton Hotel was given a makeover prior to the Three Lions' arrival. Personal touches, such as family photos, were added to each of the players' rooms to increase the feeling of familiarity. New additions at SGP ahead of the tournament included barbecue spaces, a basketball court, a pitch and putt golf area, cricket pitch and outdoor cinema as well as a new cryotherapy unit and a modified physiotherapy area.

Of the 13 pitches at SGP, it was Pitch 6 - named the Sir Bobby Charlton Pitch - where the team spent the majority of their time training. Pitch 6 is an exact replica of Wembley Stadium's Desso GrassMaster playing surface, as is Pitch 5. Both pitches mirror Wembley's 105m by 68m dimensions and have the same base composite of sand, gravel and soil topped with 20 million stitched fibres, each two centimetres apart.

While on site, players were catered for in terms of breakfast, lunch and dinner and had individualised shakes for post-training and snack stations to keep their energy levels high. Chef Omar Meziane prepared some wonderful barbeques during the tournament and ensured all the players' nutritional needs were met throughout their time at SGP with the meals and snacks he provided. Meziane served as chef for the England U20s at their successful World Cup campaign in 2017 and travelled with the senior squad to the FIFA World Cup a year later.

When the players had some downtime, they socialised over coffee, played table tennis, golf and on computer consoles. There was also some watching of boxed sets – with skipper Harry Kane revealing he caught up on the hit HBO series Game of Thrones during UEFA Euro 2020! Regular press conferences took place at SGP during the competition in which Southgate and his players spoke to the media.

With its close proximity to Wembley Stadium, England also used Tottenham Hotspur's Training Centre in Enfield to stay and train during UEFA Euro 2020 on the eve of some of their Group D matches, while they also stayed at some different central London hotels ahead of the knockout phase games.

You can see for yourself what England's players got up to at SGP during UEFA Euro 2020 by checking out a series of 'Inside Training' videos on www.youtube.com/user/fatv/videos You can watch the squad being put through their paces with warm-ups, training drills, stretching and gym sessions and getting involved with fun and games with pool volleyball, a water balloon fight and pranks from Bukayo Saka!

About St. George's Park

Opened in October 2012, St. George's Park is home to all 28 England teams. In addition to the Men's and Women's senior teams, Men's age groups from U15 through to U21 and Women's age groups from U15 to U21 use the Staffordshire-based facility, as do eight disability teams.

Ahead of an international fixture, England players will typically meet up at St. George's Park after they have played for their respective clubs the weekend prior to the first Three Lions/Lionesses game. For a summer tournament, they will usually meet up a week or so after their final domestic match of the season.

In addition to England's various teams, this world-class facility has welcomed over 150 teams to date from all over the world, and not just football, but other sports too including England Rugby Union, England Rugby League, GB Hockey, British Basketball, British Judo, British Swimming and British Rowing.

THE STORY OF HARRY KANE MBE

A combination of hard work and sheer talent has seen England captain Harry Kane become one of the best strikers in world football...

Harry Kane was born in Whipps Cross Hospital in Leytonstone, London on 28 July 1993 – the same hospital former England captain David Beckham was born some 18 years previously.

Like so many millions of boys and girls, Harry grew up loving football. Raised in Chingford, he loved to have regular kickabouts with his dad Pat and brother Charlie in a park behind their home as youngster.

Harry went to Larkswood Primary Academy before following in the footsteps of Beckham by attending Chingford Foundation School between 2004 and 2009. Like 'Becks', as well as Andros Townsend (another Leytonstone-born player who went on to wear the Three Lions), Harry played for local side Ridgeway Rovers as a kid.

The striker briefly trained with Arsenal as a youngster but was released after a year. It was at the Gunners' north London rivals, Tottenham Hotspur, where Harry was able to progress from youth to senior level. His route to the top took time. Before making his Spurs debut in a UEFA Europa League match against Heart of Midlothian in August 2011, the striker netted five times in 18 League One matches during a loan spell with Leyton Orient in 2010/11.

He was loaned to Millwall the following season and in 2012/13 he spent time with both Norwich City and Leicester City as he looked to build experience and stake a claim for inclusion in the Spurs first team.

Towards the 2013/14 season, Harry was given the opportunity to play a number of competitive matches for the north Londoners. He followed up his four goals in 19 appearances that season, with 31 strikes in 51 club appearances in 2014/15 as he truly announced himself in the colours of Spurs.

With Harry's form for the Lilywhites, it was no surprise to see England come calling. The forward had previously represented the Young Lions at U17, U19, U20 and U21 level. His senior debut came as he was introduced as a 72nd minute substitute for Wayne Rooney in a UEFA Euro 2016 qualifier at Wembley Stadium on 27 March 2015. The Three Lions were leading 3-0 when he was introduced to the game and within 79 seconds, he made it four with a far-post header. Harry had touched the ball just three times prior to his first senior international goal.

"I'm just proud," beamed Harry after his England debut. "It's a special night and definitely one I won't forget. It's what you dream of as a kid, it's a bit of a daze and I'm enjoying every minute of it."

The goals kept on flowing. Harry netted 63 times in 88 matches for Spurs in the next two seasons (2015/16 and 2016/17), as he collected the Premier League Golden Boot at the end of both of those campaigns. By the end of 2017, he had scored 12 goals in just 23 England appearances.

Harry managed his best club goal tally in 2017/18, with 41 goals in 48 competitive matches for Spurs. He carried that form into the 2018 FIFA World Cup – his second appearance at a major tournament for England, having travelled to the UEFA European Championships with the Three Lions two years earlier.

Harry's brace in England's 2-1 victory over Tunisia in the Three Lions' opening Group G fixture – which included a stoppage time winner at the end of the 90 minutes – set the tone for a marvellous tournament for player and team. He got a hat-trick in a 6-1 victory over Panama in England's second group match, before notching his sixth goal in the tournament against Colombia in the round of 16. The Three Lions (captained by Harry at the tournament) went on to reach the semi-finals and the striker collected the FIFA World Cup Golden Boot. Harry's efforts in Russia were also rewarded as he was appointed a Member of the Order of the British Empire (MBE) in the 2019 New Year Honours for services to football.

In qualifying for UEFA Euro 2020, Harry scored in all eight of England's Group A matches – netting a total of 12 times. Unsurprisingly, he was the highest-scoring player in UEFA Euro 2020 qualifying, becoming the first Englishman to net in every game in a qualifying campaign. His 12 international goals in 10 appearances in 2019 was also the joint highest tally for an England player in a single calendar year. Harry's goals in qualifying included a hat-trick against Montenegro in a 7-0 win at Wembley Stadium as he captained his country in their 1,000th international.

Harry skippered the Three Lions at the delayed UEFA Euro 2020 tournament, as England made it to the final of a major competition for this first time in 55 years. His four tournament strikes (against Germany and Denmark and a brace against Ukraine) took him to within 15 goals of levelling Wayne Rooney's all-time scoring record of 53 for England. He also cemented sixth place on the Three Lions' top all-time goal scorers list, just two short of equalling Michael Owen's tally of 40 goals in fifth.

Speaking of goal scoring records, Harry is second on Tottenham Hotspur's all-time goal scoring list. By the end of the 2020/21 season, he had scored 221 goals in 336 matches for the Lilywhites – just 45 goals shy of Jimmy Greaves' all-time club record of 266 strikes. He collected the Premier League's Golden Boot and Playmaker of the Season awards at the end of the 2020/21 campaign having managed both the most goals (23 in 35 Premier League appearances) and the most assists (14) of any player in the division.

THE STORY OF STEPH HOUGHTON MBE

From school playground kickabouts to captaining England at senior international level, Steph Houghton's football journey has been a real adventure...

Steph Houghton's journey to football stardom began kicking a ball around in the garden and park at the age of three. The future England captain's dedication to the game knew no bounds as a youngster; she took part in games on the playground of South Hetton Primary School, even when she was the only girl involved. The Durham-born defender's talent stood out as a teenager and at Sunderland's academy. It was a dream for Houghton, who was in the academy of the club she loved most.

"Sunderland are my team... I absolutely love them," she once told The FA in an interview. Having progressed through the Black Cats' academy, Houghton made her senior debut aged just 14 and spent five years with the Wearside club as

a whole, earning promotions and winning FA Young Player of the Year in 2006/07. That was when she decided to move to Leeds United. Leaving her childhood club was painful, but she was ambitious and knew that a transfer could help take her blossoming career to the next level.

Houghton spent many years representing her country as a schoolgirl and then a youth team player. Her transfer to Leeds helped her kick on, not only in the club game, but internationally too. In 2007, she made her England senior debut for the Lionesses in a 6-0 win over Russia in Milton Keynes. Transferring to Leeds cemented her position as an England player for many years to come. She also won her first trophy while in West Yorkshire: the 2010 FA Premier League Cup.

However, it was during this period that Houghton suffered two horrific injuries. She missed the 2007 FIFA Women's World Cup due to a broken leg, before damaging her cruciate ligament on the eve of UEFA Women's Euro 2009. She was determined to return and represent her country at major tournaments. Her moment would come...

It 2010, Houghton joined Arsenal, where she would spend three successful years. In just three seasons, she won seven major titles with the Gunners.

It was during her time in North London that Houghton got the opportunity to represent Team GB in an Olympics on home soil. She was in inspired form during the Games. Despite being utilised in the left-back position, the Arsenal star scored in all three of Team GB's group games. It was a tournament that ended in eventual disappointment for the hosts, who lost their quarter-final to Canada. Houghton's three goals made her Team GB's leading goal-scorer prior to Tokyo 2020. A rare piece of goalscoring history for a defender!

At the beginning of 2014, Houghton left Arsenal for Manchester City. It didn't take her long before she started winning yet more trophies at her new club. The FA WSL Cup was won in her first season. Houghton has remained at Manchester City ever since. In that time, she won one FA WSL title, three FA Women's Cups, and a further two FA WSL Cups.

In addition to her transfer to City, 2014 also saw her become England captain. The following year, she led the Lionesses to a third-place finish at the FIFA Women's World Cup in Canada and first-ever semi-final England's women had reached at the tournament. Houghton was Player of the Match as they dispatched of hosts Canada in the quarter-finals. There was more recognition for Steph in the 2016 New Year Honours list as she was appointed Member of the Order of the British Empire (MBE) for services to football.

Under Houghton's confident and assured captaincy, England have enjoyed the most successful period of their history. The Lionesses followed up their impressive showing in Canada with another inspiring run at UEFA Women's Euro 2017, reaching the semi-finals before losing to hosts and eventual winners the Netherlands. The following year, Houghton reached a significant career landmark. The girl who had grown up in Sunderland playing with the boys in the school playground was now winning her 100th England cap. It placed her name in a very short, esteemed list of the nation's best and longest-serving football players.

Houghton dedicated her 100 caps to her family. "As a professional footballer, you have a lot of sacrifices," she said. "Probably the biggest sacrifice is being away from my family and spending my time away from home. That one's for them. The career I've had so far has been down to my mum, my dad, my brother, my grandma who comes to every single game, but also my husband as well."

2019 proved another good year for Houghton and England. The team won the SheBelieves Cup for the first time. The achievement was all the more significant when you consider they overcame the likes of Brazil, Japan and hosts and reigning world champions the United States in doing so.

England reached their third consecutive tournament semi-final under Houghton's captaincy at the 2019 FIFA Women's World Cup in France. The skipper scored her 13th and most recent international goal in the Lionesses' second-round tie with Cameroon. England won that game 3-0, before knocking out Norway by the same score-line in the following round.

Following a quiet year in the women's game in 2020, owing to the COVID-19 pandemic, Houghton was set to skipper Team GB at the Olympic Games in Tokyo in 2021 (see pages 28 and 29) and the UEFA Women's European Championships in 2022 (see pages 52 and 53).

Houghton will celebrate her 34th birthday on 23 April 2022 with so many football adventures still ahead of her.

HOUGHTON

5

UEFA WOMEN'S EURO 2022 PREVIEW

The 13th edition of the UEFA Women's Championships will be hosted in England between 6 and 31 July 2022.

TOURNAMENT HISTORY

The UEFA Women's Championships took place for the first time in 1984. Back then, the four-team tournament saw the semi-finals and Final take place across two legs, with each competing nation playing a leg on home soil. England beat Denmark 3-1 on aggregate to reach the final. They were beaten 4-3 on penalties at the end of the second leg of their Final against Sweden, which had finished in a 1-1 aggregate draw.

Norway hosted and won the tournament in 1987 – a feat matched by West Germany in 1989. A unified Germany beat Norway 3-1 after extra-time in the 1991 Final while Norway's fourth consecutive Final saw them defeat hosts Italy in 1993. The two-legged structure of 1984 returned for the 1995 tournament, with Germany coming out on top. In 1997, the UEFA Women's Championships expanded to an eight-team competition.

Germany retained their trophy and went on to win the next four Euros thereafter, including the 2005 edition, which was staged in England.

From 1997 onwards, the UEFA Women's Championships took place every four years, as opposed to every two years as previously. There was further expansion of the tournament in 2009 to 12 teams and in 2017 to 16 teams.

The Netherlands, playing on home soil, ended Germany's long-standing grip on the trophy in 2017 with a 4-2 victory over Denmark in the Final. The 13th edition of the tournament was due to take place in 2021 but was delayed a year owing to the affects of the COVID-19 pandemic.

LIONESSES AT THE EUROS

England has competed in eight of the 12 previous UEFA Women's Championships with only Norway, Italy, Germany, Sweden and Denmark having competed at more tournaments.

Having finished runners-up at the 1984 tournament and fourth in 1987, the Lionesses were beaten 6-2 on aggregate by eventual competition winners Germany in the semi-finals in 1995 after an eight-year hiatus from the Euros.

England returned to the tournament in 2001, but failed to progress out of their group. The Lionesses qualified for the 2005 tournament as hosts but were again unable to qualify for the knockout phase of the competition.

Hope Powell's England were in fine form at UEFA Women's Euro 2009. A 3-2 win over Russia and a 1-1 draw with Sweden was enough to see the Lionesses make it to the quarter-finals as one of the tournament's best third-place group finishers. A brace from Eni Aluko and a further strike from Fara Williams secured a 3-2 over Finland while an extra-time winner from Jill Scott saw England to a 2-1 semi-final triumph over the Netherlands after Kelly Smith had scored during the 90 minutes. Alas, the Lionesses went down to a 6-2 defeat to Germany in the Final in Helsinki.

England were unable to get out of their group at UEFA Women's Euro 2013, but enjoyed a run to the semi-finals of the newly expanded 16-team tournament in France in 2017. Mark Sampson's side topped Group D with victories over Spain, Scotland and Portugal. A Jodie Taylor goal gave them a 1-0 triumph over the hosts before the Lionesses were beaten 3-0 by eventual winners the Netherlands in the semi-final.

THE CLASS OF 2022

Hosts **England** take their place at UEFA Women's Euro 2022 alongside 15 other nations, including current champions, the **Netherlands**, and eight-time winners **Germany**.

Other former champions appearing at UEFA Women's Euro 2022 include Norway (two-time winners in 1987 and 1993) and **Sweden,** while **Denmark** and **Italy** (finalists in 1993 and 1997) are past runners-up.

Northern Ireland, who beat Ukraine 4-1 on aggregate in the qualifying play-offs, will be making their tournament debut. The line-up is completed by **France, Belgium, Iceland, Spain, Finland, Austria, Russia** and **Switzerland**. The draw for the group phase was yet to take place at the time of publishing.

STADIUMS

UEFA Women's Euro 2022 kicks off on 6 July 2022 when England play their first Group A match at the 74,140-capacity **Old Trafford,** home of Manchester United FC. The Lionesses will also play a group game at Brighton & Hove Albion FC's **Brighton Community Stadium** on 11 July and Southampton FC's **St Mary's Stadium** on 15 July.

Brighton will host three tournament matches in total, including a quarter-final between the winner of Group A and the runner-up of Group B on 20 July. St Mary's will stage the other Group A matches not involving England on 7 and 11 July.

Group B matches will be held at **Stadium MK** in Milton Keynes and the **Brentford Community Stadium** while the setting for Group C's fixtures is Sheffield United FC's **Bramall Lane** and **Leigh Sports Village** in Leigh, Greater Manchester. Rotherham United FC's **New York Stadium**, which opened in 2012, will host Group D games along with the **Manchester City Academy Stadium**.

Brentford Community Stadium - which is the venue for the quarter-final between the winner of Group B and the runner-up of Group A on 21 July - is the newest of the tournament's stadia having opened in September 2020. The other quarter-finals will be played in Leigh and Rotherham.

Stadium MK, which will stage one of the semi-finals on 27 July, welcomed its record attendance of 30,048 for the Fiji v Uruguay match during the 2015 Rugby World Cup. The other semi-final will be played at Bramall Lane, which has existed as a sports venue since 1855.

The Final itself will take place at the 90,000-seat **Wembley Stadium** on 31 July.

WORDSEARCH

Find the eight host towns/cities that will stage matches during UEFA Women's Euro 2022.

```
M  Y  L  M  Q  B  P  G  B  K  M  N
N  A  G  X  N  K  R  Z  Z  R  I  O
S  N  N  N  K  Y  L  X  R  R  L  T
H  O  Z  C  L  O  N  D  O  N  T  P
E  T  P  Z  H  P  V  T  R  X  O  M
F  H  L  B  N  E  H  M  K  T  N  A
F  G  L  K  M  E  S  F  T  F  K  H
I  I  L  Q  R  N  J  T  H  N  E  T
E  R  C  H  L  F  T  G  E  R  Y  U
L  B  A  V  J  L  I  L  R  R  N  O
D  M  G  B  R  E  L  X  L  G  E  S
M  K  P  V  L  N  V  T  N  K  S  H
```

BRIGHTON   **MILTON KEYNES**

LEIGH   **ROTHERHAM**

LONDON   **SHEFFIELD**

MANCHESTER   **SOUTHAMPTON**

2022 FIFA WORLD CUP PREVIEW

The 22nd edition of the FIFA World Cup will be hosted in Qatar between 21 November and 18 December 2022.

TOURNAMENT HISTORY

First staged in Uruguay in 1930 with just 13 teams competing, the FIFA World Cup has grown over the decades and now features 32 nations. From 2026 onwards, 48 countries will take part in the most watched sporting event on earth.

Brazil is the most successful team in the tournament's history, having lifted the trophy on five occasions in 1958, 1962, 1970, 1994 and 2002, while Germany has won the competition four times (as West Germany in 1954, 1974 and 1990 and as a unified Germany in 2014).

The 1982 FIFA World Cup, which was staged in Spain and won by Italy, featured 24 teams for the first time while the tournament expanded to 32 teams for the 1998 FIFA World Cup, which was both hosted and won by France.

Having previously been held in Europe and the Americas, the 17th edition of the FIFA World Cup in 2002 was staged in Asia for the first time, taking place in South Korea and Japan. The first African host of the competition meanwhile was South Africa for the 2010 tournament, which was won by Spain.

In the two most recent tournaments, Germany – buoyed by a 7-1 semi-final win over hosts Brazil – lifted the trophy in 2014, while France are the reigning world champions having beaten Croatia 4-2 in Russia in 2018.

THREE LIONS AT THE WORLD CUP

England entered the FIFA World Cup for the first time in 1950 but were unable to progress out of a group containing Spain, Chile and the United States. Walter Winterbottom's side returned to the tournament four years later and topped Group 4 before being eliminated by reigning world champions Uruguay in the quarter-finals.

Mirroring their early progress in the competition, England was knocked out of the 1958 FIFA World Cup in Sweden at the group stage and made the quarter-finals in Chile 1962, before staging the tournament for the first time in 1966.

After a goalless draw with Uruguay in the opening fixture, Sir Alf Ramsey's men topped Group 1, beating Mexico and France. They then overcame Argentina and Portugal in the quarter-finals and semi-finals respectively.

The Final against West Germany was held at Wembley Stadium on 30 July 1966. In addition to a crowd of 96,924 inside the 'Home of Football', the United Kingdom's biggest-ever television audience of 32.3 million tuned in to watch the match. Helmut Haller gave West Germany the lead after just 12 minutes but Geoff Hurst equalised soon after with a header. Martin Peters put the Three Lions in front with just 13 minutes of the game remaining but Wolfgang Weber's effort late-on forced extra-time. In the added period of 30 minutes, Hurst scored twice to complete his hat-trick and a 4-2 victory for England in the country's finest sporting hour.

England's defence of the Jules Rimet Trophy ended at the quarter-final stage of the 1970 FIFA World Cup in Mexico as they were beaten 3-2 by West Germany. The Three Lions missed out on qualification for the 1974 and 1978 tournaments. They were eliminated at the second group stage in Spain in 1982, despite never losing a game. England striker Gary Lineker was the top goal scorer at the 1986 FIFA World Cup meanwhile, as Sir Bobby Robson's side reached the quarter-final of the competition where they were beaten 2-1 by a Diego Maradona-inspired Argentina.

England reached the semi-final stage of the FIFA World Cup for the first time since 1966 at Italia '90. Sir Bobby Robson's side topped a group containing the Republic of Ireland, Netherlands and Egypt before securing extra-time victories over Belgium and Cameroon in the knockout phases. The Three Lions' semi-final with

West Germany went to penalties after the Turin clash finished 1-1 after extra time and Robson's team were beaten 4-3 on spot-kicks.

Having failed to make it to the 1994 FIFA World Cup in the United States, England announced their return to the tournament in style at France '98. Michael Owen scored an incredible solo goal in the round of 16 tie against Argentina, which finished 2-2 after extra-time. Unfortunately, the Three Lions were beaten in a penalty shootout at the end of that game.

Sven-Göran Eriksson guided his England side to consecutive FIFA World Cup quarter-finals at the 2002 and 2006 tournaments, while Fabio Capello oversaw a run to the round of 16 in 2010. Memories of a disappointing group stage exit in 2014 were forgotten four years later when Gareth Southgate steered the Three Lions to the semi-finals of the competition in Russia.

Harry Kane won the Golden Boot with six goals in as many matches, while the round of 16 match against Colombia brought England's first-ever World Cup penalty shootout success (the Three Lions won 4-3 on spot-kicks after the match finished 1-1 draw after extra-time). A 2-0 win over Sweden set-up a semi-final encounter with Croatia. Kieran Trippier gave England a fifth-minute lead in that game with a curling free-kick, but an equaliser from Ivan Perišić and an extra-time winner from Mario Mandžukić saw the Three Lions' hopes of making it to their first World Cup final since 1966 dashed.

TROPHY

Between 1930 and 1970, winners of the FIFA World Cup were presented with the Jules Remit Trophy. The trophy was originally called 'victory' but was renamed in 1946 to honour then-FIFA President Jules Rimet. The 35cm high trophy famously went missing four months before the 1966 tournament, only to be found by a black and white mongrel dog called Pickles! Brazil got to keep the trophy in perpetuity following their third success in the competition in 1970.

The current FIFA World Cup Trophy was first presented to tournament winners West Germany in 1974. Designed by Italian artist Silvio Gazzaniga, the trophy is 36.5cm tall and made of 6.175km of 18 carat gold.

2022 LOWDOWN

The 2022 FIFA World Cup breaks with tradition in terms of the time of year it will be hosted – in November and December 2022 as opposed to the usual June/July schedule. This is to avoid host nation Qatar's intense summer heat.

Qatar feature in the first match of the tournament at the Al Bayt Stadium in Al Khor, which will kick off at 10am GMT on 21 November 2022. Eight stadiums will be used across five different host cities: Lusali, Al Khor, Doha, Al Rayyan and Al Wakrah. The Final will take place at the 80,000-seat Lusail Iconic Stadium at 3pm GMT on 18 December 2022.

Qualification for the tournament was still underway at the time of writing. Should England make it to Qatar, they will be competing in their 16th FIFA World Cup Finals.

CROSSWORD

Add the surnames of these current England players to complete this crossword.

ACROSS

4. The only uncapped member of England's UEFA Euro 2020 squad at the start of the tournament. Aaron _____ (8)

5. Chelsea Women's top all-time goal scorer. (5)

6. Winner of the FIFA Best Women's Player of the Year award in 2020. Lucy _____ (6)

9. Milton Keynes-born Lioness defender who has spent her entire senior club career to date with Arsenal. Leah _____ (10)

11. Manchester City midfielder who caught the eye with his bleached blond hair at UEFA Euro 2020! (5)

12. Scored England's match-winner in their opening UEFA Euro 2020 match against Croatia. Raheem _____ (8)

DOWN

1. Scored on his England debut against Wales in October 2020. Dominic _____-____ (7,5)

2. The Three Lions' captain. Harry ___ (4)

3. Briefly held the record as the European Championship's youngest player when he made his tournament debut for England against Croatia at UEFA Euro 2020. Jude _____ (10)

7. The Lionesses' captain. Steph _____ (8)

8. Collected the Bronze Boot award at the 2019 FIFA Women's World Cup. Ellen ____ (5)

10. The only current Lioness with over 150 senior caps to her name. Jill ____ (5)

NATIONAL ANTHEM

GOD SAVE THE QUEEN

God save our gracious Queen!

Long live our noble Queen!

God save the Queen!

Send her victorious,

Happy and glorious,

Long to reign over us:

God save the Queen!

QUIZ & PUZZLE ANSWERS

P36-37 GUESS THE GOAL SCORER

A) Kieran Trippier

B) Nikita Parris

C) Harry Kane

D) Ellen White

E) Jordan Pickford

F) Georgia Stanway

G) John Stones

H) Leah Williamson

P40 SPOT THE DIFFERENCE

P41 THE GOAL SCORING TRAIL: Phil Foden scores

P42-43 ENGLAND QUIZ

1) Old Trafford
2) Germany
3) Sir Alf Ramsey
4) Sheffield
5) 2015
6) Gary Lineker
7) 32
8) 48
9) Crystal Palace, Aston Villa and Middlesbrough
10) Hege Riise
11) Fara Williams
12) Lucy Bronze
13) Netherlands
14) Martyn Margetson
15) Wayne Rooney
16) Tyrone Mings
17) Jude Bellingham
18) Six
19) Sven-Göran Eriksson
20) Pickles
21) Scotland
22) An MBE (Member of the Most Excellent Order of the British Empire)
23) Kelly Smith
24) Ellen White
25) Raheem Sterling
26) Hope Powell
27) Olympics/Olympic Games
28) FIFA World Cup
29) UEFA European Championships
30) Dutch

P57 CROSSWORD

P53 WORDSEARCH

SPOT THE PLAYERS

CAN YOU SPOT THE FIVE LIONS AND FIVE LIONESSES HIDING IN THE CROWD?